ness is a treasure! Kim Maas is honest, engag-
~~l~~enging in the stories she tells. You will laugh.
~~w~~ill be inspired to press past limitations and
~~become all God~~ ~~de~~signed you to be."

Jane Hamon, author; senior leader, Vision Church
at Christian International

"*Finding Our Muchness* is a delightful inspiration and empowerment for women in ministry. In a landscape where female men-
tors and examples in ministry are often scarce, Kim Maas's book
emerges as a much-needed source of encouragement. Too often,
women find themselves compelled to adopt a male-centric style
of ministry, neglecting the unique gifts and perspectives that God
has blessed them with.

Kim addresses this gap with refreshing insight and wisdom,
offering a compelling book that celebrates the distinctive quali-
ties of women in leadership and ministry. Her work not only
acknowledges the challenges women face in this arena but also
provides a road map for embracing your true calling. *Finding Our
Muchness* is a powerful testament to the belief that women can
lead and minister authentically, embracing their God-given gifts.

This book goes beyond the ordinary, ushering in a new era of
understanding and appreciation for women in ministry. Kim's
words resonate as a call to reclaim femininity and purpose, ultimately contributing to a more diverse and enriched landscape
of leadership within the realm of ministry."

Katherine Ruonala, senior leader, Glory City Church–Brisbane

"Kim Maas's newest book is a clarion call to all women to take
their rightful place in the kingdom of God. In the pages of this
book, you will be inspired, encouraged, and exhorted to break
out of the bondage of limitations and step into your prophetic
destiny—the reality of your *muchness* in Christ."

Kris Vallotton, senior associate leader, Bethel Church, Redding,
CA; co-founder, Bethel School of Supernatural Ministry;
author of fifteen books, including *The Supernatural
Ways of Royalty* and *Uprising*

"In an era where the concept of women sharing equal ministerial roles with men in guiding Christ's flock remains controversial, I am thankful for our Pentecostal-charismatic tradition's Wesleyan heritage. Pioneers like B. T. Roberts championed the Spirit's call for women in ministry. Dr. Kim Maas, a valued voice for many, furthers this legacy. Her latest book offers profound insights and candid reflections on her own path. This work is a vital contribution to the discourse on women's roles in edifying the Church."

Bishop Mark J. Chironna, Ph.D.

"If you are looking for a current toolbox loaded with an arsenal of effective weapons, then look no further! Kim Maas has been anointed by the Holy Spirit to deliver a now word that penetrates this temporary darkness. This is not only a woman's toolbox, but it rivals any man's toolbox, because this is *His* toolbox, filled with revelation derived from the Word of God. Amen, Kim! Good job!"

James Goll, author; leader; singer; consultant; friend of God; founder, God Encounters Ministries

"Highlighting practical lessons we can learn from many of the women in Scripture, Kim Maas shows God's heart for women to flourish in their service to the Lord."

Craig S. Keener, F. M. and Ada Thompson professor of biblical studies, Asbury Theological Seminary

"It took guts to write this book, and it will take guts to read it. There are no half-Christian niceties here, no conventional pleasantries. Rightly so. Because we can flesh out the divine muchness intended for us, imitating these mothers in Israel, only as we face what they faced and suffer what they suffered. Without death, there can be no resurrection. Christ is not born without labor."

Chris E.W. Green, professor of public theology, Southeastern University

FINDING
OUR
Muchness

Books by Kim Maas

Prophetic Community
The Way of the Kingdom
Finding Our Muchness

FINDING OUR

OUR

Muchness

INHERITING
AUDACIOUS BOLDNESS
FROM
WOMEN *of the* BIBLE

KIM M. MAAS

Chosen
a division of Baker Publishing Group
Minneapolis, Minnesota

Published by Chosen Books
Minneapolis, Minnesota
ChosenBooks.com

Chosen Books is a division of
Baker Publishing Group, Grand Rapids, Michigan

Printed in the United States of America

Library of Congress Cataloging-in-Publication Data
Names: Maas, Kim M., author.
Title: Finding our muchness : inheriting audacious boldness from women of the Bible / Kim M. Maas.
Description: Minneapolis, Minnesota : Chosen Books, a division of Baker Publishing Group, [2024] | Includes bibliographical references
Identifiers: LCCN 2023045348 | ISBN 9780800799953 (paper) | ISBN 9780800763329 (casebound) | ISBN 9781493442249 (ebook)
Subjects: LCSH: Women in the Bible.
Classification: LCC BS575 .M23 2024 | DDC 220.9/2082—dc23/eng/20231207
LC record available at https://lccn.loc.gov/2023045348

Cover design by Kirk DouPonce

Baker Publishing Group publications use paper produced from sustainable forestry practices and postconsumer waste whenever possible.

24 25 26 27 28 29 30   7 6 5 4 3 2 1

To my daughters, Molly Gessica and Nicole Roxanne, and my daughter-in-law, Kimberly Ann, who inspire me every day with their beauty, boldness, and brilliance. Your resilience in the face of adversity, your love for your family, friends, and those in need of healing, and your willingness to grow and stretch in your understanding of who you were created to be makes me so very proud of the women you are. I love you so, so much!

And to all those

- Who are ready to find their *muchness*;
- Who are feeling the sting of the accuser shouting, "IMPOSTER!";
- Who are done struggling with being "not hardly" the one they were created to be;
- Who are ready to put on armor and take up sword to slay the Jabberwocky[1];
- Who are destined to declare, by the power of the Spirit, to the world:

"My name is (Insert-name-here).

My Father has a dream, and He never lets anyone stop Him.

I AM HIS DAUGHTER!"

CONTENTS

FOREWORD

BY CINDY JACOBS

Kim Maas has written a powerful book that is timely for the exact moment we find ourselves living in. I have heard several prophetic voices give the word that this is a season in history when women are arising to be a voice to their generation. One cannot be a voice without recognizing that there is so much more to each woman than they realize! This book will expand your understanding of the powerful abilities and talents God has provided for you.

I resonated with Kim's stories of when people would stand up and shout that we were heretics for preaching the Gospel as women. I have also heard stories of women Pentecostal pioneers who had to duck for cover when bullets were flying through their meetings because of their faith. In those days, being a Spirit-filled woman preacher was not for the faint of heart!

We stand upon the shoulders of great women in all spheres of society who have gone before us. Women who have gone to nations and made history!

Kim has chosen several such women to highlight, who went from living an ordinary life to the "muchness" this book is all about. She gives unique points and insights about a personal favorite of mine, Deborah. Deborah literally saved her people when their country was in ruin and occupied. If we think we have it rough culturally, she ruled in a time when women had no rights. It is astounding to me that she became a judge and ruler.

Some of the other women Kim writes about are the daughters of Zelophehad. These biblical women affected the laws of inheritance to this day! I am so glad!

This book will bridge the generations. Its pages are full of truths that gave me fresh courage to stand in my own personal calling. Kim Maas has done all of us women a favor by writing it! Enjoy!

Cindy Jacobs
Generals International

FOREWORD

BY PATRICIA KING

Dr. Kim Maas is bold in faith and love, intelligent, beautiful inside and out, and willing to be fully transparent regarding her journey and discoveries. As a woman in frontline ministry, she has faced many challenges and has gloriously overcome them.

This is more than a book—it is a mentorship manual for YOU! As you read through the chapters you will be invited to discover the fullness of all God has destined for you to fulfill. You are not an ordinary human being—you are a supernatural being in Christ, and there is much about YOU that God wants you to discover.

Throughout biblical and Church history, we note many brave, faith-filled, and courageous women who brought light to the darkness, hope to the hopeless, order to chaos, and solutions to problems. They discovered that God was greater than any challenge they faced and any obstacle in their way. They discovered their "muchness." Have you discovered yours yet?

My favorite woman in the Bible is Deborah. She lived during challenging and oppressed years due to the disobedience of

God's people. It was in this time of unrest and hardship, however, that Deborah was called and set into place as an instrument that would aid in bringing about a turnaround for her nation.

She would have faced the same resistance many leaders experience today—you cannot be on the front lines and avoid demonic assaults and attacks from the carnal flesh of the human race, and sadly, even the flesh of fellow believers. Like others, I'm sure she was tempted with feelings of uncertainty and doubt. What gave her the courage to stand, persevere, and gain the victory? What gave her the fortitude to overcome every temptation and receive confidence to obey all the Lord called her to?

I believe it was because she found her muchness.

Many years ago, I came to a deep place of conviction and revelation that introduced me to my personal muchness. I was staring point blank at personal failures, inadequacies, and disappointments. During that season, I felt small, incapable, and attacked on every side. As brutal as that season was, that was when the greatest revelation of my journey in Christ filled every part of my being: "God + Nothing = Everything I Need." What a relief! I had everything I needed to face every battle, every disappointment, every challenge, and every invitation from the Holy Spirit. I discovered my muchness not only for that season but for all time.

God is not a respecter of persons. He is available to every one of His children, and He is always what we need in every circumstance. He will always be our MUCHNESS.

As you read, you will discover a number of keys as you glean from the lives of women who have gone before. You will be mentored and called to discover your muchness. Enjoy the book. Enjoy the journey.

Patricia King
Author, minister, media host, and producer

ACKNOWLEDGMENTS

Myriads of women have gone before me, many even now walk beside me, and innumerable more will come after me. They walk out their faith with courage, tenacity, vulnerability, honesty, humility, and resilience. They are heroes who inspire and spur me on.

Some lived a lifetime or two before me and will never know my name, yet still they influence me: Joan de Arc, Sojourner Truth, Harriet Tubman, Phoebe Palmer, Hannah Whithall Smith, Maria Woodworth-Etter, Aimee Semple McPherson, and Kathryn Kuhlman. They leap from the pages of history to lap at my heart like tongues of fire until I thirst near to death to experience the Spirit as they did. They faced limits and opposition I will never know. They answered to God alone and fulfilled the call on their lives. Thank you.

Some in my own time have pioneered the way ahead, then reached back to give me and thousands of others wise counsel, prophetic direction, and prayer. Cindy Jacobs prophesied words over me that have fueled forward momentum at three significant and strategic times in my life. Over tea in her parlor, she announced the Lord said it was time to "write the book," and she committed to write the foreword. I wrote the book. She wrote the foreword. Cindy, thank you.

Dr. Jeannette Storms (Mama Nettie), who mentored me during my seminary studies, is another pioneer who reached her hand out to take hold of mine in one of the most important and painful moments in my life. Early one morning, three weeks after my precious mom died, the phone rang. "Kim," she began, "the Lord woke me this morning and told me to call you immediately to tell you that, though I can never replace your mother, I am to offer to be your spiritual mother. I promise that you will never be without a mother who prays for you as long as I am alive. I will love you, support you, and be available to you for counsel and comfort if you want this." I accepted with snotty sobs. Dr. Jeannette Storms is an apostolic leader who planted churches in three nations and has ministered in power for more than sixty years. Mama Nettie, I can never thank you enough. You have made a difference in my life.

Some women have known me before "calling" was in my vocabulary. They believed me when I told them I had been visited by God, and they continue to be with me every step of the way. We have cheered, championed, and loved one another through times of favor, promotion, darkness, pruning, warfare, and crisis of every kind. They are the epitome of what it means to be girlfriends. Degna Horton, Karyn Roy-Smith, and Anne-Marie Warner, thank you.

Some women in my life have laid down their lives in prayer to see me through this book. Jenna, Amber, Marci, Jenimar, Fish, Tangie, Rochelle, Kelly, Sheryl, and the rest: I couldn't have done this without you. Thank you.

One woman saw potential in me as an author when I wasn't one yet. It wasn't until meeting Kim Bangs that writing books would materialize. Kim, you have helped me see what I could not see, which is one of your most excellent gifts. You are a prophet and a gift to the Body of Christ, to authors, and to the world. Thank you for being a gift to me.

I have mentioned the women, but there are also men to whom I am deeply indebted. The love of my life—my husband, Mike—is my greatest cheerleader. His wisdom and prophetic insight have helped me continue to move forward. His love and strength have given me a place to rest when I have been weary. His jokes have kept me laughing even when heaviness threatens to steal my joy. Mr. Maas, I love you forever.

To my spiritual fathers, Dr. Randy Clark and Blaine Cook, and brothers, Dr. Alan Hawkins, Dr. Nick Gough, and Dr. Rodney Hogue, thank you for your love and friendship, for seeing what the Lord was doing in my life, for adding your yes and amen, for releasing impartation from your life to mine, and for inviting me to minister alongside you. I am forever grateful for all I have received in theological and ministerial practice. You have taught me patience, humility, wisdom, and soundness in ministry while expecting and cooperating with the move of the Spirit in power.

Thanks to my former pastor, Reggie Mercado, who dared hire me in my first pastoral role and gave me freedom to lead, prophesy, and preach in full view of men and women on staff and in the pews.

Special thanks go to Dr. Chris E.W. Green. I took a risk to ask you to be a reader for this book when you barely knew me. I asked you to walk alongside me as I wrote and to help me stay within solid theological exegetical boundaries while telling the compelling stories of these women. I asked you to help me stretch in the craft of storytelling in ways faithful to Scripture. You have. And in the process, I believe we have become friends, for which

I am grateful. Thank you for all the time, conversations, and insights you offered me so generously amid your heavy schedule and responsibilities. You never made me feel as if I was a bother or that you regretted saying yes. I have grown because of our theological discussions and your encouragement to imaginatively engage Scripture. *I am looking forward to more conversations and a long friendship.*

INTRODUCTION

When I was a young girl, I did not know I was powerful. I did not know I had the power to change my life, my relationships, my world, and the world around me. I did not know it because I was kept from knowing it by all the unspoken rules and unnamed pressures that shape the lives of women in our world. Like so many others, I came to believe deep down in my bones that I had to live with a broken heart, broken relationships, and a broken world. But then I met Jesus and His Holy Spirit. He changed my mind from the heart out. He changed my world. And He filled me with the power of the Holy Spirit to bring that same change everywhere He sends me.

Everywhere I go, all around the world, I talk to women who are hungry for more of the goodness they can sense God intends for them. They want to see God move in and through their lives. They want to participate in advancing the Kingdom of God. This is no surprise. God is bringing revival to the nations, exactly as He has promised. There is a revival move of God coming, and within that move is another move—a move of God among women. All kinds of women. In all kinds of situations and stations of life.

The women's movement began many years ago, coming in waves, moved by the winds of the Spirit that are blowing over the face of the deep. In contrast, it is easy to see that another wave is already forming and gathering great strength. The feminist movement has captured the attention and involvement of many young women in my country. The radical feminist movement sanctions and even at times joins in the oppression of men, the victimization of the unborn, and the persecution of the followers of Christ. That is not the movement of which I, and prophets around the world, are speaking.

When one oppressed people group rises out of their oppression only to turn and crush another people group with the power they have gained, God cannot be in it. It isn't who He is. In other words, it is not in His nature as the life-giving Creator, the good, good Father who has made us for the abundant life of righteousness, peace, and joy in the Holy Spirit.

I was ministering in a tornado shelter during the 2017 Women's March in D.C. In a rare moment of abandonment, I wrote an emotional response on Facebook. Here is an excerpt:

> I have been ministering for years to women whose lives have been wrecked by broken promises, financial disparities, educational inequalities, governmental injustice, infidelity and betrayal, sexual and emotional abuse, and trauma from every kind of evil. I have wept with and for them. I have stood with and for them. I have suffered with and for them. I have witnessed many, but not enough, healed, restored, and set free. When I heard the speeches at the [Women's March], I was disappointed. I was disappointed because I can feel a women's movement coming on the horizon and I welcome it . . . but this is not it. This is not what I've been waiting for.
>
> The right to abort a child is not the main issue facing women in the world today where most women have no right to choose

20

not to be mutilated, not to be burned, not to be married at nine years old, not to be raped, not to be sex trafficked, not to be left out to die because they were born female, and not to be enslaved rather than sent to school.

I'm looking for something greater, nobler . . . something worthy of my gender and the evil perpetrated against us all over the world since Eve.

I'm looking for those who have voices of influence and dignity and wisdom that cannot be ignored and that carry into all nations to protect women's bodies from rape and torture and forced sexual exploitation. I'm looking for a movement that makes way for little girls all over the world to grow up with a choice of schools and future endeavor. I'm looking for a movement of women that will protect the choice of women to marry when they are truly of age if and when they desire such a union. I'm looking for a movement of women who conduct themselves with respect, brilliance, dignity, and eloquence. Women who understand that to create a real movement that transforms culture and shapes history requires real guts to take real risks and make real sacrifices on behalf of real women everywhere.

Did you get that last part? *To create a real movement that transforms culture and shapes history requires real guts to take real risks and make real sacrifices on behalf of real women everywhere.* Guts. Risks. Sacrifices. The change God wants from us and for us and through us cannot come apart from us being courageous and acting boldly.

My all-time favorite prophetic movie is *Alice in Wonderland*— the one from 2010 with Johnny Depp.[1] There are three main characters: the Red and White Queens (sisters) and Alice. The Red Queen has been ridiculed her whole life for her big head. Unable to accept herself and unable to get past what she feels is a personal injustice, she grabs for illegitimate power and self-promotion, destroying all hope of ever gaining what she truly desires most—to be loved and valued.

The White Queen is blessed with beauty, talent, and favor. She becomes the target of her sister's bitter insecurity and envy, who falsely and unfairly imprisons her so that she may shine. The kingdom, once ruled by the generous and gracious White Queen, is now ruled by the cruel and controlling Red Queen. The kingdom of Underland suffers violence and devastation.

Alice has forgotten who she is. She used to have dreams. She used to practice believing six impossible things before breakfast. She has forgotten she is a champion of the kingdom, created to slay the terrible dragon. Yet, tragically, when the kingdom desperately needs her, she emphatically declares, "I'm not slaying anything."[2]

Standing amidst the land devastated by fire and destruction, the Mad Hatter speaks. "You don't slay . . . You're not the same as you were before. You were much more muchier. You've lost your muchness."[3]

He points his finger at her belly, her middle, her "guts" and "backbone," where the strength of identity must be, diagnosing her. "In there; something is missing!"[4]

Muchness. *That* is what this book is about—finding our muchness. Getting back what is missing: the power, force, or essence with the confidence of who God says that we are and what He has called us to do that got lost in the confusion, troubles, and uncertainties of life. We were not born to find a comfortable place and stay there. We were born to be champions, to push back the darkness, and to advance the Kingdom. We are not called to envy, jealousy, and back-biting power struggles, but to stand together as a force to be reckoned with, defying the gods of this age.

And we can have it if we want it. Deuteronomy 6:5 says we are to "love the LORD your God with all your heart and with all your soul and with all your *me'od.*" *Me'od* is Hebrew for "muchness." It is literally "very" or "very much" and connotes your total capacity, the fullness of who you are, with all your God-given power and force.[5] Think about it. If you and I were not created with muchness, God would not command us to love Him with it. It is who we are, what is in us, and how we love God and accomplish everything for which we were created.

God is about to move in unprecedented ways among the people group called *female.* Women will be released into their God-designed purpose in unprecedented numbers. Some of us are being called to preach. Some of us are being called to write books. Some of us are being called to the nations. Some of us are being called to plant churches. Some of us are being called back to school. Some of us are being called to government and politics. Some of us are being called to reform the social welfare and child protective services on behalf of children. Some of us are being called to reform the mental health care system. Some of us are being called to reform the education system. Some of us are being called to advocate for women, the unborn, sex-trafficked victims, child brides, the lost, the forgotten, and the voiceless. The list is endless. There is room for all of us because there is a need for each of us. We are living in a strategic time in history.

At strategic times in salvation history, God has chosen women and empowered them with His Spirit to carry out His will in extraordinary ways. He chose Mary to give birth to the Savior. He chose another Mary to be the first apostle to proclaim the Good News of His resurrection. And He chose women in the early church to pastor, teach, and proclaim the gospel. Women were co-workers with the apostle Paul and joint-heirs together with Christ and their brothers in the faith. And at the dawn of the greatest revival since the Day of Pentecost, He bestowed on a humble woman—Agnes Ozman—the privilege and responsibility of being the first to experience and proclaim the Pentecostal baptism of the Spirit in the 20th century. Throughout the century, He called countless women and empowered them to fulfill both humble and high-profile assignments. In the 20th century, Spirit-filled women began to discover that these women were not exceptions to God's plan, but instead were His prototypes for God's woman.[6]

Each chapter of this book is really a small book in a larger frame. I will tell you up front I do not begin each chapter with a clever anecdote meant to thrill or convince you that by three, or five, or twelve easy steps you can reach the pinnacle of success. I don't begin each chapter in any particular way at all. Each woman and each story is unique. Sometimes I may begin rather abruptly, jumping right in, feeling an urgency to get to the good part, the part where the Holy Spirit is highlighting how this woman's courage is averting crisis, saving her people, and always moving the Kingdom forward. Sometimes I tell the story in a more narrative fashion, allowing the Holy Spirit to tell the stories without added noise or nicety in ways He highlights them. Sometimes I tell the story in pragmatic fashion, allowing the Holy Spirit to highlight practical issues and applications for our lives. In every telling, my heart is to tell these real-life stories in ways that honor the lives of the women in every generation—yours and mine included.

I have done my best to follow my hunches, nudged by the Lord through prayer and thoughtful reflection, for the placement of each story as makes the most sense to me. I ask you, however, to follow yours in the reading of them—you know best both where you are and what you most need in the moment. Pray, and be free to read them in or out of order, but I would ask this—read with your makeup off—ready to get down into the dirty with each character, relishing and savoring the stories and life messages therein. Each tells the story of a woman who had to come to terms with her identity and found her muchness. They are real flesh-and-blood women, but their beauty is not just skin deep. They are women who advanced the Kingdom courageously and cunningly, defying cultural, religious, and gender traditions, as well as the systems of the world that were arrayed against them. They were champions.

Every one of them had to take a risk to become who they were meant to be and accomplish what they were called to do. To take that risk, they had to find their muchness! You will have to do the same. If that makes you nervous, just think about Jesus. He took a risk on all of us. Before we were born, He knew us. Before we were born, He planned a purpose for our lives. He gave His body and His blood to secure it for us.

So, I ask you, *Are you ready to find your muchness?* I know that for some that sounds threatening, intimidating. But you do not need to be afraid. If you can hear the call to move into your muchness, then you can be confident that the Spirit is empowering you to answer that call. Would you be reading these words right now if this were not true?

1

Throw Out the Bondwoman!

SARAH'S STORY

· GENESIS 12–17, 21 ·

> For it is written that Abraham had two sons: the one by a
> bondwoman, the other by a freewoman. . . . Nevertheless what
> does the Scripture say? "Cast out the bondwoman and her son,
> for the son of the bondwoman shall not be heir with the son
> of the freewoman."
>
> Galatians 4:22, 30 NKJV

*S*INKING FACE DOWN on the carpet in a puddle of
snot and tears, I confessed my doubts, fear, and insecurity to three astonished friends. Hadn't I believed the word of
the Lord and left everything—my nursing career, my comfort,

the neatly planned life—to serve the call of God that had suddenly and unexpectedly broken in those many years ago? I was serving the Church full-time. I went to school and studied hard to earn a master's and then a doctoral degree. I had diligently prepared for this very moment. After nineteen long years, the door abruptly opened to the nations, and where before I had stood before handfuls and hundreds, I now found myself standing before thousands.

Suddenly, I felt like an imposter. Suddenly, I was intensely intimidated and afraid. I was sure that at any moment, the people who invited me into this position would discover that I was unqualified and send me home ashamed. I was afraid I was not intelligent enough, pretty enough, articulate enough, anointed enough.

I struggled. Hard. I cried. A lot. I prayed. Hard. Did I mention I cried a lot? You know, the snotty, ugly cry. I was filled with an almost-paralyzing fear before every ministry engagement. This went on for months. Then I discovered during this time that there is a real thing called Imposter Syndrome. Psychologists tell us, "[t]he imposter syndrome is a psychological term referring to a pattern of behavior where people doubt their accomplishments and have a persistent, often internalized fear of being exposed as a fraud."[1]

I started asking the Lord, "Where did this come from? When did this begin? How did it take root in me?" One day in prayer, the Lord brought to mind an old memory. I was in the third grade. A man came to our school, and some students were dismissed from regular classes to meet with the man. I was one of those students. I wasn't told why I was chosen, but I was given a pass to meet with him. Over a few days, I got to tell the man stories, draw pictures, and answer many questions. I had so much fun. I felt *special*. At the end of those days, the man brought my mom into the office and spoke with her. That evening, my mom brought me into the kitchen and spoke with me.

Mom explained that the man at school was testing students to see if they were eligible for the gifted and talented program. My teacher had felt I showed signs of giftedness and sent me for testing. You had to score a certain number of points to qualify. I came up short by half a point. In other words, I was not gifted and talented. "But," Mom encouraged, "the man said if you work really hard, you will always be able to keep up with the gifted and talented students." Mom wanted the best for me.

It suddenly all made sense. As a third grader, I was disqualified from being allowed into the gifted and talented program. The teacher thought I was gifted, but on close examination, it was decided that I was not. From that moment on, I worked really hard and kept up a good performance to be counted among those who were gifted and talented. Yet, in my heart, I knew the truth. I did not belong among those who were gifted. I was half a point short. I did not measure up. I was an imposter in my own eyes, driven by the pressure to perform and haunted by a deep-rooted fear and insecurity that I would be exposed and put to shame because of my lack.

I needed freedom if I was going to fulfill the call on my life. I needed to be freed from the fear of myself, because that fear was keeping me from sharing God's freedom with others. I needed deliverance out of my fears into my muchness. And I am not alone.

A Model of Faith

In the book of Galatians, Paul uses typology to juxtapose two Old Testament women, Sarah and Hagar. Typology uses a person or event from the Old Testament as a type or prefiguring of another person or event in the New Testament to explain or make a theological point. In this passage, Paul points out that bondage and freedom cannot coexist.

Sarah is portrayed as a free woman. She is the one whose life became the instrument through which the prophetic promise would be fulfilled and the Kingdom would be furthered. She lived by faith and received the impossible. She demonstrates that the covenant promise of God comes to us by faith—not dependent on human initiative and ingenuity, ethnicity, looks, brilliance and education, sociopolitical standing, or financial status. It comes by the Spirit, through whom the impossible becomes possible. It comes by grace through faith. The author of Hebrews remembers Sarah as a model of faith: "By faith Sarah herself received power to conceive, even when she was past the age, since she considered him faithful who had promised."[2]

Can we stop right here for just a moment? You may be thinking, *I'm too old now. It's too late for me to be a part of whatever women's movement thing she is going to tell me about.* I would like to say with great tenderness and passion that you are never too old until you are with Jesus in eternity. God is moving in our generation, and a generation in the Spirit is not an age group. It is an era of time. Now is that time. You, too, are being called out by God. It is time to believe and receive the power to conceive at whatever age you are.

"Therefore, from one man . . . were born descendants as many as the stars of heaven."[3] This one man is Abraham. Abraham is the man who left everything to follow God, not knowing where he was going, simply because God told him to go.[4] Sarah was Abraham's wife. She was *not* just a tagalong. She, too, left everything to follow God's word. She, too, received the prophetic word of promise. Just as Abraham was to become the father of nations, Sarah was to become the mother of nations. She was the chosen vessel through which the covenant would be birthed, and the nation of Israel, the people God chose in His wisdom to bring His blessing to all the peoples of the world, would come into being.

Facing Reality

I love that when the Holy Spirit inspired Paul and the author of Hebrews to write Sarah's memorial in the New Testament, they did not remember a Sarah who struggled with unbelief, the sense of her own inadequacy and identity, or the impossibility of God's promise for her life. It gives me hope that I will be remembered for becoming a freewoman of faith, not a struggling bondwoman. Or, more honestly, I hope my struggles are remembered in the light of my freedom and faith. The truth is that Sarah's story is not all glimmering bravado and confidence. Sarah's journey to becoming who she was created to be is a pattern that can be found in the lives of the great men and women of faith in Scripture. The pattern is a growth process initiated by a prophetic promise—a word of the Lord. This is important because identifying the pattern allows us to identify where we are in our own process. It isn't over yet. God is not finished with us.

Sarah's story begins all the way back in the book of Genesis when she was called by a different name.[5] The story starts with an introduction. We are told Abram[6] took a wife named Sarai who "was barren; she had no child."[7] This is a startling, stinging statement. Sarai, whose name suggests royalty, is introduced to us as not only childless, but also barren. The writer wants us to know her by what has not happened to her, and what she is not capable of doing. She cannot fulfill the calling of her own name.

Why does Scripture introduce her this way? It seems rude, even cruel. Imagine you are at a party, church, or a family gathering, and here comes Abram. You have never met his wife, and someone says, "I'd like you to meet Abram's wife, Sarai; she can't have children." *Ouch.* Yes, it seems a bit startling. It does seem rude.

Introductions in Scripture are important. They introduce facts that are keys to understanding the revelation buried in the narrative. Sarah's barrenness is meant to be upsetting because the whole story of Abraham centers around a prophetic promise that his offspring will become a great nation.

God releases a prophetic word of promise to Abraham about descendants that outnumber the sands of the sea, and Sarah is unable to have children. It seems cruel, but it is the beginning of something new in her life—the beginning of the growth process. A prophetic word of the Lord, a prophetic call and promise, *first* brings a confrontation with reality.

The prophetic word magnifies her limitations. In Sarah's case, the limitation is barrenness. Sarah does not have it in her to make this happen. She will not be able to fake it, force it, work it, or think it into being. This will be God's doing in her life only if she believes and yields to it. God alone will be glorified, not her hard work or performance. Faith believes God. It takes Him at His word even when there seems no reason to hope for such a thing.[8]

Whenever a prophetic promise comes to us, it meets us right where we are physically, emotionally, spiritually, relationally, and even financially. It brings us face-to-face with the reality of our lives and limitations. What was Sarah's reality? She was, according to the flesh, unable to have children. Sarah lived a life limited by her barrenness, and because of her limitation, she also lived a life of reproach. Reproach is a mixture of shame, criticism, disgrace, and disapproval. In her time and culture, barrenness was not just sad; it meant being an outcast. This is the reality of Sarah's life.

Seen as cursed by God, she lives as an object of reproach. Cultural expectations are failed because Sarah couldn't do what women were expected to do. Relational expectations are failed because her family line has a prophetic promise dependent on progeny, and she can't deliver. Religious expectations are failed because she is the primary obstacle to the fulfillment of a divine promise. Because of her barrenness, Sarah is not seen for who she is.

Barrenness was Sarah's reality, as far as her body was concerned, but not her identity. When we believe barrenness or any other limitation, circumstance, experience, wound, or past sin defines us, we take it to ourselves as an identity. Anytime our perceptions of ourselves don't match God's perceptions of us, we are not standing in our true identity. We are not free women.

In my years as a pastor, I spent many hours counseling people. I often encountered women who could not receive even the smallest compliment. They would make an excuse to deflect the praise so that it was not received. Most of them had experienced being criticized or humiliated. They had had many experiences of not being valued or honored. Somewhere along the way, that pattern of experience had been internalized, taken to heart, and as a result, became core to their identity. They believed they were worthless, or at least worth less. To receive a compliment, to take to heart the truth of you that only others can see, you must believe you have worth and are worthy of receiving praise. These women, because of what they had suffered, believed a lie formed by their lifelong circumstance. Worthlessness, which once had been only a series of experiences, now had become an identity, and every situation, conversation, and relationship was redefined by it. As their pastor, I recognized that there would be no gift, no compliment, no friendship, no love that could be genuinely received unless true identity could be restored.

Sarah was barren. Her culture and community did not see her as God saw her. She did not yet see herself as God saw her, but God still chose her to give birth to the promise. He would use her human limitations for His glory and bring Sarah into her true identity. Sarah's circumstances were a setup for a miracle in which God would be glorified!

The Testing

Remember Joseph? He is the young man who dreamed a prophetic dream about being raised to governmental authority over his brothers, father, and mother. His future looked bright, but the days following the dream were dark and painful.

> When [God] summoned a famine on the land and broke all supply of bread, he had sent a man ahead of them, Joseph, who was sold as a slave. His feet were hurt with fetters; his neck was put in a collar of iron; until what he had said came to pass, the word of the LORD tested him.
>
> Psalm 105:16–19

After coming face-to-face with the reality of our lives and limitations, a word of the Lord will bring testing. Whenever God releases a prophetic word of promise, the question is, Will we believe to see the fulfillment of the promise even through a time of testing? Why? Because from the beginning in the Garden, we are to be the people who live by every word that "proceeds from the mouth of God."[9] This requires faith. Faith is believing the revelation and obeying through the testing to its fulfillment.

When we think of testing, we often think of punishment. Challenges, difficulties, and struggles can feel like punishment. What if we stood above the circumstances from a vantage point with the Holy Spirit and allowed Him to show us what He is doing and what we are supposed to learn? What is my point? Testing is not for punishment but for the purpose of *revelation*.

Testing allows us to *see* how we measure possibility. The prophetic word of the Lord comes to us, and we immediately measure the possibility of it coming to pass against our natural talent, abilities, and resources. We are, of course, going to come up short! Who can accomplish God-sized promises but God? Our limitations and flaws are suddenly magnified, so we determine it is impossible for the prophetic promise to come to pass. It just can't happen. No way. No how. Not now. Not ever.

But God measures the possibility of a prophetic promise coming to pass in our lives against Himself. His abilities. His resources. He is the measure of all possibility. With God, all things are possible. Nothing is impossible with God. Nothing. Nada. Not one thing.

Testing allows us to *see* what we believe. (I'm using the word *see* here to imply revelation. Something hidden that God desires to reveal.) What we believe is revealed by our default responses to a word of the Lord. Think about it. Moses said, "I can't speak." Jeremiah said, "I'm too young." Gideon said, "I'm too small; the least and the weakest of all." Sarah said, "I'm barren, and I'm too old." I said, "I'm a woman. I'm just a mom from Moorpark." Our default responses reveal in whom we have put our faith. When possibility is measured by our ability and resources—as opposed to God's—our faith is in ourselves.

Testing also creates a crisis. A crisis is a time when a situation becomes dangerous, unstable, difficult, or painful. In crisis, decisive action must be taken to avoid complete disaster or breakdown. In other words, a crisis brings pressure to perform.

Sarah has been living with the prophetic promise for some time now. A lot has happened, including a move, two rescues, and a war, which tells us it has been years. After all this, God revisits Abraham and reiterates the prophetic promise about offspring. Abraham candidly and honestly blames God for not giving him a child and suggests his servant will be his heir. God does not scold or rebuke Abraham. God says no, "This man shall not be your heir; your very own son shall be your heir."[10] Now comes a most famous and important declaration about faith: "And [Abraham] believed the LORD, and he counted it to him as righteousness."[11] Beautiful! Stupendous! Hooray! Except that a few verses later, we read that Sarah is still barren and "had borne him no children."[12]

Can you feel it? The word is testing them. The situation is heating up and magnifying their limits, making them the focus. The crisis is created, and with it comes an opportunity to respond. Imagine how Sarah feels. She knows her history and her inability to produce children and meet the expectations of her culture, family, husband, and self. *She* is the obstacle to her family's blessing. *She* is the object of reproach. *She* is the one standing in the way of their blessed future. *She* can't stand it anymore and becomes motivated by fear and unbelief and succumbs to the pressure to perform, fix it, or *do something*.[13]

In the midst of testing at the moment of crisis, Sarah speaks. Until now, she has been silent in the text. For years she has silently waited for the promise to come to pass. Perhaps she believed for a time, but when conception did not take place, she resigned herself to barrenness, comforting herself by believing that God had not actually spoken. Maybe she believed God did not want to lift the curse on her life, and shame stole her voice. In any case, hearing the promise brought up again, she could not remain in resignation and silence any longer.

What emerges is a little sequence that is very important because it surfaces again a bit later. Words are full of meaning in Scripture. They reveal the heart and what we believe.[14] Voice is often equated with authority, power, and influence. Loss of voice occurs when we come under oppression and abuse by others, or when we abuse our power and authority. What we believe, we speak. What we speak influences.

Sarah speaks, "Behold now, the LORD has prevented me from bearing children. Go in to my servant; it may be that I shall obtain children by her."[15] We are shocked. She is asking Abraham to have sexual relations with her servant to fulfill the prophetic promise of God. What she says is culturally acceptable, even a duty, for one who is barren. She has responded by doing what was legal in the culture but illegal in the Spirit. It is a natural (aka worldly or fleshly) attempt at achieving a supernatural promise.

What is happening here? She has spoken as the barren wife. She has spoken in agreement with a barren identity, a *false* identity. She uses her position and authority to manipulate circumstances under the pressure to perform.

Abraham listens to the voice of Sarah.[16] He thought it was a reasonable solution. It might work. What is interesting is that God is silent. He was not consulted in the matter, though He is the One who made the promise. When we give in to the pressure to perform, we often make decisions based on reason alone. The people around us may even agree with our decision and we may not be stopped by God. This, however, does not equal His approval. It simply means that sometimes God will allow us to

make decisions that threaten our destiny to bring revelation to
our table.

Reaping Consequences

Sarah's speech reaps consequences. When Sarah agreed with her
false identity and acted under pressure to perform it, it opened
the door to Hagar.

Hagar is her slave. Hagar is an Egyptian. Why is that fact important? Moses is recounting this story in the book of Genesis. Moses
is the prophet deliverer featured in the book of Exodus. What is the
book of Exodus about? It recounts the great Old Testament story of
the deliverance of the people of Israel from their bondage to *Egypt*.
Their deliverance is called the exodus. The exodus is another type
(remember typology). It foreshadows the Gospel story of how Jesus
will deliver His people from bondage to sin and death. Egypt, like
Hagar, is used in the New Testament to represent slavery, bondage,
sin, flesh—whatever exalts itself above God comes between God
and us. It twists, deceives, and undermines our true freedom and
identity in Christ, thus hindering the call on our lives.

Giving in to the pressure to perform costs Ṣarah her place and
her influence. It brings a reversal of position. The bondwoman,
Hagar, becomes the wife—the conceiver—and Sarah remains barren, now enslaved with jealousy and resentment. Women in this
ancient culture gained honor and power through childbearing.
Conception elevated their social status. Hagar had performed well
and produced the heir apparent. She is promoted. Contempt is
now added to the life of reproach Sarah bore.[17] Reproach is disapproval. Contempt is disrespect and disdain, a disdaining of authority structures. It brings division to the household. Sarah's place and
authority in the family are undermined.[18] Egypt has gained power.

Listen, woman of God, Egypt is waiting to gain power in your life to usurp your authority. It craves dominion and control. Let's not be deceived. When we come into agreement with a false identity, it gains power in every area of our life.

And now, Sarah has become abusive.[19] Do you see what is happening? This woman of promise is reduced to a victim. She becomes jealous, resentful, and blaming, and when handed back her power, she is abusive, lashing out against her Egyptian slave (as later, Egyptians will lash out against their Hebrew slaves—Sarah's own descendants). Too often, we who have experienced some kind of barrenness, betrayal, injustice, or rejection harbor unresolved anger from wounds that have never healed. We then make decisions out of our woundedness. When the result is more loss, less power and influence, we turn to hurting or abusing others.

At this moment in history, God desires to give us back our power, authority, and influence. He desires for us to know how to wield our power for good. He desires to give us a voice that will be heard, change lives, and shift the course of history. But our voice cannot issue out of a false identity, victim mentality, or bitter root in our lives. Unhealed wounds and unresolved issues are a threat to the prophetic promises over our lives. Time to take a closer look at any place in our lives where this is happening. Take responsibility for our part, knowing all is *never* lost. Mistakes are learning opportunities. They reveal where we need God's intervention, healing, and restoration.

The Redefining Moment

Hagar gave birth to Ishmael, and life went on. Abraham was 86 years old when Ishmael was born. At the age of 99, God breaks in once more and speaks to Abraham about the promise of an heir.

Wait, what? Hadn't Ishmael fulfilled that? To everyone's surprise, he hadn't.

> And God said to Abraham, "As for Sarai your wife, you shall not call her name Sarai, but Sarah shall be her name. I will bless her, and moreover, I will give you a son by her. I will bless her, and she shall become nations; kings of peoples shall come from her."
>
> Genesis 17:15–16

How kind is God? At just the moment when we are sure all is lost and we have gone too far in the wrong direction to receive what God has promised, He breaks in to allow us to become our true selves. It is the next step in the process. A word of the Lord—the prophetic call and promise—brings us to a defining moment that redefines who we are and calls us to adjust our lives according to His word.

God begins by changing her name. A name in the culture in which Sarah lived represented the character and purpose of the person. *Sarai* meant "princess." *Sarah*, according to the Word of the Lord, means "queen" or "*mother of nations*." God reestablishes Sarah's true identity and calling. She is a mother of nations called to stand beside Abraham, the father of nations.

The prophetic promise and call were not just for Abraham. Sarah was not just a tagalong. She was receiving an invitation to partnership in the Kingdom. Blessing, favor, and supernatural empowerment would come with her identity and call. She is not called to be the *obstacle* to the fulfillment of the promise. If she believes God, He will empower her to be the *instrument* of fulfillment, an equal partner in the work that must be done, a co-laborer and joint heir.

I want you to hear me now. There is an important revelation to receive, and it is this: God gives no blessing or favor *to a false identity.* There is only pressure to perform; pressure to meet every false expectation other people will have for us. Aren't we ready to be free from that? *All blessing, favor, and Holy Spirit empowerment come with our identity and call in Christ Jesus if we will believe.*

The tension is thick as we sit on the edge of our seats to see how Sarah will respond. She responds with doubt and sarcasm. Sarah laughs.[20] Immediately, she is confronted by the Lord: "Why did Sarah laugh and say, 'Shall I indeed bear a child, now that I am old?'"[21] And then God asks a question that is not a question at all. It is rhetorical, meaning that it requires a certain fixed answer. "Is anything too hard for Me?" In other words, God is declaring once and for all, "No. There is nothing too hard for Me."

The Hebrew word for *hard* in this passage can be translated as "wonderful."[22] God is asking Sarah, "Is anything too wonderful for Me to do for you? Am I good enough, in your understanding of Me, to do this wonderful thing in, for, and through you? Is it bigger than Me, better than Me, greater than what I am capable of? Do you believe I love you enough to do this on your behalf?"

This is it. Sarah has come to her defining moment. She must decide whether or not she is going to believe and adjust her life according to what He has spoken. God has issued Sarah an invitation to be redefined.

There comes a moment in the life of anyone who dares to follow Jesus when we either stand and believe to the fulfillment of the promise or we shrink back. Isaiah warns, "If you do not stand firm in your faith, you will not stand at all."[23] The writer of Hebrews exhorts us:

> Therefore do not throw away your confidence, which has a great reward. For you have need of endurance, so that when you have done the will of God you may receive what is promised. For, "Yet

a little while, and the coming one will come and will not delay; but my righteous one shall live by faith, and if he shrinks back, my soul has no pleasure in him." But we are not of those who shrink back and are destroyed.

Hebrews 10:35–39

Sarah accepts the invitation. How do I know? She says nothing. But she has not lost her voice. This is not a return to her earlier silence. It is resolve. Sarah speaks with her actions. She conceived a son, meaning that after years of barrenness, staggering disappointment and pain, and the evaporation of physical capacity through menopause, Sarah had sexual relations with Abraham. As women, we can understand the meaning of this.

So many of us, myself included, have been through the pain of miscarriage or barrenness. She is past the age of childbearing. For ninety-plus years, she has been barren. For ninety-plus years, month after month, she has suffered the disappointment of not being able to conceive. How many times did she dare hope, only to have it dashed into shame-filled pieces? How often did Abraham approach her in intimacy, and she was filled with dread to relive the agony again?

Now she is not only barren, but she is also menopausal. We can only imagine the courage it took for this woman to lay herself down, open herself up, and make herself vulnerable one more time to offer such worship unto God. This precious and costly act of worship, this faith-filled vulnerability to the word of the Lord, releases the power and favor of God over her life, and she conceives.

She gives birth to Isaac, and Sarah is no longer the barren woman. She is the mother of the promise. She is the mother of nations. Her vision, perspective, and speech are redefined. She *sees* everything in a new way. She no longer lives under oppression and the curse of a false identity; she is free. What did this freedom mean to her? Certainly, it meant joy in returning to her status as wife, mother, and matriarch of the family. Certainly, it meant living without shame. Freedom meant all of this, and it meant living out her God-given power and identity with the responsibility to watch over and steward what God had given into her care. Promises once birthed pass and grow up in a world of conflict and under threat. Sarah, in her newness, must be courageous and cunning as she walks in her calling.

Hagar and Ishmael are still a part of her life. On the day she weans Isaac, while they are throwing him a party, Sarah *sees* Ishmael "laughing."[24] The Hebrew word used in this verse, *tsachaq*, can be translated as "playing" or "mocking."[25] We don't know which it is, but we know that Sarah has a fierce reaction.

Throw Out the Bondwoman

"Cast out this slave woman with her son, for the son of this slave woman shall not be heir with my son Isaac,"[26] she demands, using words used to cast out a demon. There will be no tolerance or compromise. There is to be a complete severance. She will not allow the promises of God, or her family, to be enslaved, corrupted, mocked, stolen, or destroyed. She has taken back her voice, with all the power and authority that belongs to her.

This time when Sarah speaks, Abraham questions, and God speaks.

> And the thing was very displeasing to Abraham on account of his son. But God said to Abraham, "Be not displeased because of the boy and because of your slave woman. Whatever Sarah says

43

to you, do as she tells you, for through Isaac shall your offspring
be named."

Genesis 21:11–12

This was Abraham's son, and he had an affection for him. What
Sarah demanded was that Abraham disinherit his firstborn son. It
was not simply against tradition; it was illegal in the culture. Sarah
understood. She understood that Ishmael, as the firstborn, could
lay claim to Abraham's wealth and property by cultural laws and
that Egypt could steal the God-given promises, the God-given
inheritance, and the God-given name.

At this critical juncture, the Lord backs up this woman amid
a patriarchal society. "Whatever Sarah says to you, do as she
tells you." This should sound familiar! This is what Mary essentially says to the servants at the wedding at Cana: "Whatever
He [Jesus] says to you, do it."[27] Sarah is a type of Christ in this
story. God has taken this marginalized woman with a past full of
reproach, shame, and barrenness and has given her governmental authority to lead her tribe protecting His promises for their l
ives.

The pattern is complete. The growth process has come to fulfillment. Sarah is no longer the barren woman. She is Sarah, the
mother of nations. She has taken back her voice and her silence
and has stepped into her place as a matriarch standing beside a
patriarch for the Kingdom of God. She is the freewoman.

Remember Who You Are

Yet, her story does not end there. Thousands of years later, we,
like countless women from generation to generation, are reading her story. Like Moses, I am retelling the story of Sarah's life

44

to remind you of who you are. I am here to remind you of the heritage, identity, and freedom that is already yours, paid for in full by Jesus Christ. I am here to remind you of the call on your life. I am here to remind you that the Holy Spirit has been poured out, and you are a new creation. I am here to remind you that you belong to a people of the Spirit with miracle-working power and authority. I am here to remind you to take back your voice, your power, and your authority in Christ—all of which are gifts to you and for others—and use them as they were purposed to be used, which is to deliver God's people from their bondage so that the prophetic promises of God are preserved in their lives. We are Sarah's daughters, Sarah's sisters. With her and like her, we are called to a muchness that moves us to laugh, not in mockery but in joy.

God is calling us out to rise up. We are no longer to live as though we are unworthy, without value and something to offer, no longer believing we are without authority and power to make a difference, no longer intimidated to remain silent over injustice. We are no longer to be enslaved to cultural dictates, religious discriminations, or personal indecision. God is calling us to *throw out the bondwoman*—the slavery, bondage, and false identities that keep us "not hardly" ourselves.

Remembering Hagar

There is more to Hagar's story. In telling Sarah's story above, Hagar and Ishmael have been portrayed as a type of Egypt. Like Paul in Galatians, the portrayal is typology for the purpose of seeing into the storyline; however, like Sarah, Hagar is not just a typological lesson. She is a real person who found herself in a foreign land serving a family who served a foreign God unrecognized in her homeland.

If you notice, when we read the stories of Sarah and Hagar, our heart goes out to Hagar. After all, none of what happened was her idea, by her own volition or decision, or under her control. She was a woman without a voice, power, or authority. She had enjoyed momentary privilege and chafed at being treated as a slave. Hadn't she been "given" into the arms of Sarah's husband at Sarah's behest? Her becoming pregnant was part of a plan conceived by her mistress. But when the plan came to birth, it conceived more than a child. It also gave birth to trouble, abuse, and rejection. She and her son were cast out. This wasn't part of the plan as she had imagined it.

We feel compassion, and maybe a bit of anger, for her and her son, who were abandoned to die in the wilderness. Then we notice that Scripture presents her, the Egyptian slave, as the first to name God! Scripture is honoring her, assuring us that God cares for her and her son. How can this be? Hagar is a pagan, a foreigner, a servant, a nobody. Her son is not the son of promise. Abraham and Sarah's act of casting them out was sanctioned by God.

By this we expect that God would not care for or about them. Yet God does not abandon them in the wilderness. He had promised to make a nation of her son.[28] Her status was not prohibitive to God. He honors His promise to her and allows her to honor Him by giving Him a name—the God who sees and sustains her. And He surely is the God who sees. He sees Sarah. He sees Hagar. He sees every one of us.

Perhaps you identify more with Hagar than you do with Sarah. You do not feel so much the need to cast out your false identity as you feel you have been cast out by others because they misjudged you and assumed you and your gifts were a threat to them and their future. God sees you. He has a plan and a promise for you, and He will fulfill it even if you are in the wilderness.

What's more, the truth is that in Christ, Sarah and Hagar, Israel and Egypt, Jew and Gentile, master and slave, are reconciled. At the foot of the cross they embrace as sisters. With *muchness*.

2

Get in Position!

THE STORY OF THREE WIDOWS

• RUTH 1 •

And they came to Bethlehem at the beginning of barley harvest.

Ruth 1:22

*W*ITH GOD, the end is only the beginning. Thanks to the power of the Creator Spirit—the power that brought all things into being and that led Israel out of Egypt and raised Jesus from the dead—we are never left without hope. When it all seems finished, over, and done, we will be positioned to receive a redemptive harvest for our life and the lives of others if we are willing to risk starting over. I know three women who lost everything: their dreams, their partnerships, and the legacy they were building. It all came to a crashing end. It was the beginning of their story.

We all experience crisis and tragedy when God seems absent, or worse. We begin to think that maybe He doesn't see what is happening. *Perhaps He doesn't care. Maybe this is His will for my life, my "cross to bear," so to speak. Maybe (this is what is worse) He is not real.* It can be a bitter, confusing time.

I have learned from my own experience and the pages of Scripture that God is not afraid of our pain or of what we do because we are in pain. God is the Great Physician, and no dis-ease in us frightens Him or leaves Him at a loss. God is the Master Teacher, so the questions that arise in us never back Him into a corner. God is a Friend closer than any brother; He remains with us in our trouble, a very present help.

Whether we see it or not, He is always working. The psalmist says He never slumbers nor sleeps and is always near to help. Paul tells us He is working in and through everything to bring good out of it in our lives.[1] I love how Anglican bishop N. T. Wright puts it: "The world is still groaning, and we with it; but God is with us in this groaning and will bring it out for good."[2] The groaning is the groaning of childbirth.

If you are groaning right now, I know where you are. I am groaning, too. Some days I have been tempted to quit. I have felt that I can't labor anymore. I can't breathe through the contractions. I can't keep pushing. My groans sometimes fade into sighs, then into silent tears. I have been stretched, squeezed, pressured, challenged, tested, and tried. James says encountering various trials tests our faith and produces endurance.[3] Hebrews urges us to remember the former days when we endured great conflict and never to throw away our confidence, because we need endurance.[4]

I think it helps to know God is working in us the ability to endure because we are living in a time of accelerated change. This change is setting things up for a time of Kingdom harvest. This change will reposition us to be a part of it all.

The story of Naomi, Ruth, and Orpah is about courage in hardship, moving forward, and how God orchestrates ordinary lives to bring about His extraordinary plans. It is a Cinderella story of sorts, but there is no fairy godmother turning pumpkins into carriages. There are no supernatural occurrences at all, yet everything that happens is supernatural because working in and through the story is an invisible God whose providence and sovereignty bring about His divine redemptive plan. The supernatural is often cloaked in the tattered garments of humanity.

As Carolyn Custis James writes about the book of Ruth, "God casts a vision of breathtaking proportions for how his kingdom is moving forward through the efforts of women—*ordinary* women like most of us."[5] The book of Ruth is a true story about a time like ours and women like us and God, who has our times in His hands.

What Time Was It for Ruth?

The final verse in Judges, just before we turn the page and get to Ruth, is sobering: "In those days there was no king in Israel. Everyone did what was right in his own eyes."[6] Corporately, it was the time of the judges—a time of lawless moral decline. There was violence, chaos, and upheaval in every area of communal life—in the cultural, religious, economic, and political arenas. There were no righteous leaders. Corruption, self-centeredness, and arrogance ruled the day.

There was a famine in the land alluding to another deadly spiral of apostasy and idolatry. The people of God had turned away

50

from Him and were suffering the consequences of great hardship. Yet, there is hope. Hidden in the mention of famine, according to Robert Hubbard, is another allusion pointing to "the biblical pattern that famines, despite tragic appearances, often advance God's plan for his people."[7]

And here is where we must begin, on the edge of hope at the bitter end.

The Bitter End

For the three women, the opening lines of their story are a tell-all of their circumstances.

> In the days when the judges ruled there was a famine in the land, and a man of Bethlehem in Judah went to sojourn in the country of Moab, he and his wife and his two sons. The name of the man was Elimelech and the name of his wife Naomi, and the names of his two sons were Mahlon and Chilion. They were Ephrathites from Bethlehem in Judah. They went into the country of Moab and remained there. But Elimelech, the husband of Naomi, died, and she was left with her two sons. These took Moabite wives; the name of the one was Orpah and the name of the other Ruth. They lived there about ten years, and both Mahlon and Chilion died, so that the woman was left without her two sons and her husband.[8]

I don't want you to miss the drama of these opening lines, lest you miss the depth of despair and the impossible odds they are facing. When Elimelech, whose name means "God is King," dies, he dies outside the boundaries of his covenant inheritance. This means that the birthright, land, possessions, and property he owned in their homeland, waiting for them when the famine was over, is gone. Naomi is left with nothing. Her hope of survival now lies with her sons. Then, as quickly as the shift to her sons is made, it all dies—the men, the provision, the hopes, and the dreams of any fertile future. Are you getting this?

What's more, in a patriarchal culture, having husbands and sons determines your worth. Naomi's sons, though married for ten years, had no children born to them before they died. No husband, no sons, no grandsons—no worth. The women, Naomi, Ruth, and Orpah, are left barren and widowed, without protection, provision, or a prospective future. It is a dire situation. Their fate seems sealed. They have come to a dead end. In time, this family will cease to exist.

Fresh Bread

It is in the dead places God brings revival. Spurgeon interprets revival in this way: "To live again, to receive again a life which has almost expired; to rekindle into a flame the vital spark which was nearly extinguished."[9] Death seems inescapable for our three widows. There is famine in the land of Judah. There is no bread. Where there is no bread, there is no life.

Suddenly, revival! A testimony of God's tender care and provision is heard in the fields of Moab.[10] God has visited His people in Bethlehem! He has returned bread to the house of bread, whose barren shelves had left its people starving and driven families to foreign lands for survival.

The visitation is a testimony. It is a testimony of God's covenant faithfulness and loving-kindness toward His people. It is revelation. God is revealing or introducing something new to us (information, direction, intervention), and with it comes the opportunity to engage our faith by hearing and responding to the fresh revelation. Faith is responding to divine revelation. It is hearing and turning with obedience and endurance through times of testing according to what is heard.

A change has come. We scoot to the edge of our seats, anticipating what the women will do. Will they turn and go to the place where God has returned bread? Will they risk starting over or stay in the place where everything, except the grain fields, has died? Their husbands started this project, it was their vision, but it didn't work out as planned.

Amid grief, the women will have to make room for a new vision to move forward out of the dead place into the place where there is fresh bread and new life. For each of us, there will be times when we must stop investing our energy, time, or money in what has stopped producing fruit and is no longer viable. It may mean stepping away from unhealthy or abusive relationships, old ways of doing things, addictive cycles, and sick family patterns. We cannot keep doing the same thing repeatedly and expect different results! We will have to resist the temptation to stay where things are familiar and instead turn and go where there is fresh bread. We will have to listen to the voice of God, decide to start over, and go where God is presently working.

That is more complicated than it seems. I know. Sometimes, we become heartsick and decide to give up hope. We check out emotionally. As hard as it is, staying emotionally present in pain allows God to bring healing.

I experienced a time when the pain of abuse I suffered, some disappointments I experienced, and several personal failures I navigated seemed so big I could not face them. I could not meet them head-on and overcome them. I didn't know I could. I didn't know if I had it in me or if the tools were within my reach. I was tired. I was young and inexperienced. I was afraid.

I made a decision. I decided that I would not feel the pressure or the pain. I can't say how conscious or subconscious this resolution was, but I can say that the choice not to feel worked for a long time. I got married, I had children, and I went to church. It seemed to be working for me.

After a while, however, some signs began to shout at me, and I knew I would not be able to continue to remain numb or neutral over the issues in my life. I started taking more drastic measures to mask the increasing emotional distress I was in. That resulted in an eating disorder. Though I did not want others to know, the person I was really hiding it all from was me. I'd have moments when anger would spill out onto my children for simple mishaps, or I would fall into weeping uncontrollably. I did know God. I did pray. I was mad, and I thought, *Why doesn't He do something? Why doesn't He come and rescue me? Doesn't He love me?*

No lightning bolt from heaven, no booming voice out of the clouds, only a stirring so small it was barely discernible, but there came a growing hunger for a different life, a life with color. Author Henry Cloud said, "We change our behavior when the pain of staying the same becomes greater than the pain of changing."[11]

Have you noticed that the greatest changes sometimes come from the smallest decisions? When I decided not to feel the pain and not to speak about what hurt, disappointed, or frightened me, I simply became numb. I didn't feel at all. As I chose to open my heart and tell its story, suddenly the days were no longer gray and numb. They became dark and stormy.

I experienced grief and sorrow for a season. The Man acquainted with suffering stood with me to help bear my grief and carry my sorrow in ways I had not understood He would. He gave me the strength to stand face-to-face with all that threatened my heart with failure. One day, the dark season came to an end.

The darkness lifted, and light suffused my soul. I felt the hint of warmth and the possibility of laughter again. I felt a fragile confidence and tentative happiness.

The point is, I had not known that to choose not to feel pain would mean that I chose not to feel joy. I had not understood that refusing grief, anger, or sorrow did not bring peace, but rather a disconnection with emotion of all kinds, including mirth, happiness, and passion. I learned that to have joy in my life, I have to be willing to experience pain. Emotion does not rule my life; it is not the driver of the bus. But it does give it rich texture and color. I can enter joyful and painful experiences with others because I have learned how to embrace my history without my life ending or being derailed. I have learned how to stay present and remain hopeful regardless of what I am feeling.

Hope is related to faith. Faith is the substance of things hoped for and the evidence of things not seen.[12] Hope is an expectation of the good things to come, things that are known to be good in faith. Faith is the substance of what is hoped for because what is expected is not yet manifested, not yet seen. In other words, we believe it is coming and want it to come because we are sure that it is good. Hope dies when we stop believing there is anything good ahead of us.

Maybe your hope is on life support right now due to the warfare, losses, unfulfilled expectations, and hardships you have endured. You have not given up completely, but you are barely hanging on. The Lord will come with mouth-to-mouth resuscitation to revive your hope because He loves you, He is faithful, and He knows you need faith for this time. We all need faith.

Remember, faith is hearing and turning in obedience with endurance according to what is heard. The voice of fresh revelation has been heard in the wasteland of the lives of Ruth, Naomi, and

Orpah. Something new has been introduced. There is a sudden change brought about by God. There is bread. The famine is over. God is moving on behalf of His people!

Each of these three women has been given an opportunity to respond. They respond by rising up, gathering all they have, and setting out for the place where God is visiting His people with bread.[13] It is a good beginning, but soon they will hear competing voices that will test their faith.

Competing Voices

The three widows have turned and set out on a journey to return to the place of divine presence and provision. The words *turn* and *return* are used twelve times in the first chapter of Ruth. This is significant. Repeated words are used in Scripture to emphasize what the Spirit is saying. *Turn* and *return* are words of repentance pointing to a change of mind and heart, resulting in changed behavior or direction. The turns each of these women take will give us a glimpse into their thinking and what they believe about what they heard. Where they place their faith will bear fruit in a direction that affects the trajectory of their future. They turn in response to what they hear.

From the beginning, in the Garden of Eden, the testing of faith has come from competing voices. Whose voice will we hear? Whose voice will we trust? Whose word will we put our faith in? The drama played out in the Garden, and in every story of man since, is to answer the question, Will man live by every word that comes from the mouth of God?

Adam and Eve were given a word of instruction, direction, and provision from God. It was divine revelation. They were to put their faith in God and His word. The devil, who is shrewder than any other creature, appears in the Garden and speaks a different word. His was a competing voice vying for their attention and drawing their faith away from God. They put their faith in the devil's word, and it led them out of the place of divine presence and provision.

The first voice declaring a testimony of divine visitation in Bethlehem has been heard. The journey of faith has begun. Two verses into their journey, a new voice is introduced.

> But Naomi said to her two daughters-in-law, "Go, return each of you to her mother's house. May the LORD deal kindly with you, as you have dealt with the dead and with me. The LORD grant that you may find rest, each of you in the house of her husband!" Then she kissed them, and they lifted up their voices and wept.[14]

Can you hear it? It is the voice of reason. The voice of reason makes good sense. It resounds with the culture. It is practical and sensible. Naomi is not being unkind. She is aware of what a Moabite widow will face in her homeland. She understands the cost her Moabite daughters-in-law will pay to follow the voice of God and follow her back to Bethlehem. Culturally, they will face perpetual singleness, racism, and gender inequality. She urges them to return to their mother's house, where betrothals are made. It is practical and reasonable advice—go back to your family and find a new husband among your people. The voice of reason shouts, "Be sensible and do what is practical." If we put our faith only in what the voice of reason tells us, we won't hope for anything beyond what we see. We won't take risks.

When neither daughter-in-law repents of their decision to follow her and the testimony of God's presence and provision, we hear another voice. The voice of bitterness.

"Turn back, my daughters; why will you go with me? Have I yet sons in my womb that they may become your husbands? Turn back, my daughters; go your way, for I am too old to have a husband. If I should say I have hope, even if I should have a husband this night and should bear sons, would you therefore wait till they were grown? Would you therefore refrain from marrying? No, my daughters, for it is exceedingly bitter to me for your sake that the hand of the LORD has gone out against me."[15]

The voice of bitterness sounds like a warning to turn back or get hurt. Bitterness in Scripture is a reaction to the experience of suffering in harsh circumstances or perceived unfairness.[16] Upon arrival in Bethlehem, Naomi will introduce herself as Mara, which means "bitter." She will tell her old friends that she went away full and has returned empty. In Naomi's defense, Carolyn Custis James writes, "Death cruelly cheated her of the joys of motherhood and the honor due a mother of two sons . . . this final chapter of her story promised nothing more than running out the clock. Naomi was going home—not to live again but to die."[17]

The voice of bitterness shouts, "Go back! The curse on me will come upon your life, too. Go back! There is nothing in it for you if you go with me. Don't think you have any future if you go any further. You will be better off returning to your old life. You will only get hurt and incur more loss if you follow the voice of revelation." The voice of bitterness always cautions you to protect yourself. It is a voice of unresolved grief and anger. It is full of resentment, at least when it has fully grown.

Bitterness narrows vision and blames God and those around you. It distorts faith, rejects hope, disowns joy, and distrusts love. It defiles our speech, behavior, and relationships because we see and react to everything through a bitter filter. If we put our faith in what the voice of bitterness tells us, we will never trust anyone—not even God.

Though able to resist the voice of reason, Orpah cannot resist the voice of bitterness. She listens, and her vision narrows so that she cannot see any future moving forward. She turns back. She repents of her decision to go where there is bread and turns to her old way of life to look for her future in the past. She rejects the promise for the familiar. What is the fruit of her repentance? Sadly, she disappears from the pages of Scripture, and her voice is not heard again.

Listening to the voice of bitterness will always result in turning back from faith in God's promises. Eventually, the divine vision with prophetic promises that once burned brightly in our hearts will narrow until there is nothing left. Once clear and strong, filled with the hope of the Gospel of the Kingdom, our voice will be emptied of its authority. This is why Hebrews warns us to allow "no 'root of bitterness'" to spring up and cause trouble because it will ultimately cause its host and those who listen to them to turn away from their faith in Christ.[18]

After Orpah turns back, we hear the final competing voice. The voice of conformity.

> Then they lifted up their voices and wept again. And Orpah kissed her mother-in-law, but Ruth clung to her. And she said, "See, your sister-in-law has gone back to her people and to her gods; return after your sister-in-law."[19]

The voice of conformity casts doubts on your decision using tactics like comparison, fear of failure and humiliation, peer pressure, and others to make you comply with its demands. The insidious voice of conformity sounds like this: "Don't be stupid.

Look at everyone else; they have made the right decision. What do you think you are doing? You are going to make a fool of yourself. Be like them."

Ruth is left clinging to Naomi. At this moment, standing alone without support, encouragement, or assurance, Naomi uses the harsh voice of conformity to convince her to save herself from the life that surely awaits her in Judah as a barren, widowed foreigner. It will cost her everything to move forward in faith. Her family, her culture, her homeland, her religion. She will have to start completely over. She has lost so much already, and watching her stand before Naomi, we hold our breath wondering if she will take such a great risk.

Ruth's Turn

For the first time in our story, we hear Ruth's voice. With unbridled passion and formidable resolve, she not only refuses to repent of her decision but forsakes all else. She binds herself by covenantal promise to Naomi and the God who provides bread, whatever may come—including death.

> "Do not urge me to leave you or to return from following you. For where you go I will go, and where you lodge I will lodge. Your people shall be my people, and your God my God. Where you die I will die, and there will I be buried. May the LORD do so to me and more also if anything but death parts me from you."[20]

In our culture it is hard to recognize the radical nature of what Ruth has done. She has committed to value a relationship with Naomi in a culture where your worth as a woman was determined by your relationship with men, and where being widowed and barren labeled you accursed. She has placed her faith in the God of a people with whom she will be considered an outsider, looked down upon, and perhaps abused. She is risking her life to follow this woman and this God.

This is faith. Ruth stood alone before God and man and made a courageous choice. She heard the voices of reason, bitterness, and conformity, but she did not listen or obey. She chose to put her faith in another voice, the voice of revelation. She believed God, Naomi's God, the God of Israel. She longs to go where there is bread, bread that God alone can provide. She chose to turn away from what she once knew to turn toward a new, unknown future with Naomi and Naomi's God.

Isn't this what Abraham did when God called him to leave his country and his family to go to a land he had never been to and did not know? Scripture says that by faith Abraham obeyed and left without knowing where it would lead him.[21] Don't miss this. Ruth is being portrayed as a woman of extraordinary faith, comparable to the great patriarch Abraham. The Holy Spirit is holding her up to the light for all to see and follow. The Holy Spirit is honoring this ordinary girl as an example of faith among men, though she is not a man, in an era when culture valued men. God has always valued women.

What is the fruit of Ruth's turning? She will meet her God and the man who will redeem her past by accepting her marriage proposal. She will be instrumental in bringing Naomi a personal revival and be promoted in the Kingdom, giving birth to God's Kingdom purposes and becoming the mother of Obed, who was the father of King David in the line of Christ. When Orpah turned back, her voice was silenced, and she vanishes from the story, but Ruth's life and voice will go on to figure prominently in the rest of the book.

Naomi's Turn

The moment Ruth lifted her voice in faith, risking everything, the testing stopped. Naomi said no more. The attention is now on her. No words are heard between them as they journey on to Bethlehem. The silence is broken by town gossip. "And when they came to Bethlehem, the whole town was stirred because of them. And the women said, 'Is this Naomi?'"[22] To which Naomi responds in the voice of bitterness:

> "Do not call me Naomi; call me Mara, for the Almighty has dealt very bitterly with me. I went away full, and the LORD has brought me back empty. Why call me Naomi, when the LORD has testified against me and the Almighty has brought calamity upon me?"[23]

Naomi is bitter, without doubt. She even renamed herself "bitter," using the name Mara. Yet notice where she is. She has returned. Whether it is desperation or faith, or faith working through desperation, she has returned to Bethlehem. Ironically, the name *Bethlehem* means the "house of bread." It is ironic because, if you remember, what Naomi heard in the field was that God had visited His people in Bethlehem and had given them bread. Famine had emptied the house of bread of its substance and provision. Now, bread again filled the house. Technically, because she responded to the revelation she heard in the field, she has returned by faith. This is important because Scripture is revealing to us that bitterness is not equal to unbelief.

A Word about Bitterness

Bitterness is not good, but it is not a disqualification. How do I know? Follow the name. At the beginning of our story, Naomi is

introduced as, well, Naomi, meaning "pleasant" or "abundance."
A name to the Hebrews connotes identity. Often names prophetically describe divine heritage and inheritance. Naomi's life was meant to be plentiful. Yet, even as she is introduced, we are told of her bitter loss and tragedy.

We can imagine how her time of loss and great grief would bring a sense of loss of identity: her role of wife and mother shattered by death, her sense of community and belonging in culture, and her faith lost in geographical separation. *Who am I? What contribution can I have? Who will remember my name?* All are common questions asked by those who live through incredible loss and trauma. It is not, therefore, inconceivable that she would spiral into bitterness and reject her own name, feeling her identity is lost.

Bitterness, as further defined, is caused by hard life experiences of immense pain, shame, and sometimes profound mental and spiritual anguish. Scripture lists several experiences that give way to bitterness: barrenness and infertility (see 1 Samuel), an unfulfilled death wish (see Job 3:20), family crisis (see Genesis 27), exploitation and deprivation (see Esther 4:1), personal suffering and hardship, and a hostile and precarious life situation (see Psalm 64:3).

When Naomi describes herself as empty, she is agreeing with the culture of her day, which measured her worth in men: having husband and sons. When she accuses God of emptying her life of all value and meaning, she is agreeing with her culture, which labels barren and widowed women as accursed. Bitterness narrows vision, blames God and others, resorts to reason, distorts faith, rejects hope, disowns joy, and distrusts love. Naomi cannot find any evidence of God's goodness or love despite Ruth's commitment to stay by her side for the whole of her young life.

Bitterness is disfiguring and distorting, but it can be healed, and it does not necessitate disqualification from a life in Christ or the fulfillment of a call. How do I know? Follow the name! Here is the very next verse: "So *Naomi* returned, and Ruth the Moabite her daughter-in-law with her, who returned from the country of Moab."[24]

The Spirit-inspired text preserves her identity. She is never once called Mara by the Holy Spirit or by Ruth or anyone else in the book of Ruth. God never repents of giving identity, gifts, and callings to His people.[25]

Our Kingdom identity is seen in eternity by God. He sees us as we are, even when we don't see ourselves that way. Though Naomi's identity is marred by the bitterness of her life experiences, and she defines herself by her emotional reaction, her true identity is not changed. Her name and identity are kept intact by God Himself. He never calls her by any other name.

It will be her choices moving forward that will determine whether she will fulfill her Kingdom purpose and become who God has created her to be. It will not be her circumstances, the culture, or the enemy. God has spoken her name over her and covenanted to be with her because she is one of His own. In this first chapter, and in every chapter of Ruth, she makes a right turn, choosing to return in the direction of the voice of revelation, even in all her bitterness.

What is the fruit of her returning? She will experience personal renewal and will guide Ruth, devising a strategy to reveal the man who will redeem and marry her. She will finally receive the restoration of her inheritance in the birth of a grandson.

Now we find ourselves at the end of our story, the final verse of chapter 1 in the book of Ruth. We have heard many voices and followed the turns each of our three widows has taken. Naomi and Ruth made right turns by choosing relationship with God and one another. They did not exchange the promise for the familiar—they kept moving forward. Their right turns resulted in being positioned for harvest!

Positioned for Harvest

All along, it hasn't only been about the place where we would arrive, but the timing. "And they came to Bethlehem at the beginning of barley harvest."[26] Sadly, only two arrive. Not everyone will choose to risk starting over after so much loss and suffering.

Barley harvest is a signpost pointing to events of divine intervention in which the people of God will experience joy, restoration, productivity, and singing.[27] It is symbolic of the faithfulness and loving-kindness of God, who blesses His people with abundance and fulfillment. It signals a change of season or a new season. The barley harvest leads to the wheat harvest. These coincide with the seasons of Passover and Pentecost, foreshadowing our salvation, deliverance from death, and empowerment with the Holy Spirit.

Again, I have to tell you that not everyone will choose to risk starting over after experiencing so much loss and suffering. Those who do will find themselves positioned for a fresh outpouring of God's presence and ready to participate in a new move of God.

Remember, with God, the God of cross and resurrection, the end is only the beginning.

3

Speak Up

THE STORY OF FIVE SISTERS

· NUMBERS 27:1–8 ·

They speak right, give them a possession.[1]

*T*HIS LIFE IS NOT FAIR. There are imbalances that are just part of what I call the human experience. In my generation, we were told, even as children, that we must come to terms with it and move on. I thought lots of things were unfair. I thought it unfair that my big brother was in charge when Mom was working, primarily and especially when he would chase me around the house, threatening to "pound" me for not obeying his dictates. Looking back, I see what a heavy responsibility was placed on him.

I thought it unfair that I didn't get to be a cheerleader in high school. They decided that year to have a smaller squad of six even after the student body voted in seven, and I was number seven. I joined the swim team instead and learned to compete with confidence.

I thought it unfair when, at nineteen years old, my then fiancé was caught sleeping around three weeks before our wedding day. I married Mr. Maas instead and we have, as of this writing, 43 years, three children, and six grandchildren together. I am glad for it.

Some of what we think of as unfair is simply a matter of perspective. Some of what we think of as unfair, in fact, is. There are things that we should be given that are kept from us and things that we should not suffer that are done to us. We are not only sinners, but we are also sinned against. We live in a fallen world that has been impacted by sin and corrupted by demonic influence. Thus, life will be unfair at times, and we will suffer consequences that are not due to our own failings.

But we have a God who is just and loving beyond our imagination, who watches over us as we experience these things that test our character, who is with us in them, all the while actively molding us into people who are more and more like Him.

Sometimes, things are more than unfair; they are completely wrong, totally not right. They are unjust. And something being unjust is very different from it being simply unfair. Children sold into slavery, for example, is not right. Girls made to marry grown men at nine or ten is not right. Bride burning[2]—setting your wife on fire because she does not please you or because her dad didn't pay you enough to marry her—is not right. Even something less horrific but still painful and life-altering, like my biological father abandoning my mom and three-year-old me for another woman, never to return, is not right. These are things that my close friend Anne-Marie would say "ought not be so."

Sometimes the cultural or familial status quo is the thing that is not right. Though it is or has always been the norm, it is unjust. Sometimes, because it has been the norm for so long, those within the twisted system are unaware of how not right it is. Sometimes they think of it as "just the way things are." Sometimes they may even know it "ought not be so" but haven't the strength, the courage—the *muchness*—to speak up and stand against it. But, sometimes, there is somebody who does.

In the book of Numbers, we will meet five sisters who stood together when things in their world were truly not fair and not right. Their story is highlighted in Scripture in a book of counting in which girls didn't seem to count. Yet, in highlighting their story, we can rest assured that God thinks otherwise. He makes sure His Word is written so that we can discover what He wants us to know. And He wants us to know, *that we know, that we know* (an old Pentecostal way of saying it is settled down deep and sealed by the Holy Spirit) that we not only count, but we also have a part to play in the unfolding history of His Kingdom.

He also wants us to know that living a life that counts will require *muchness*—courage and cunning—because sometimes we will come up against things that are more than unfair; they are not right. In the midst of that injustice, oppression, or bias, we will need to take a stand together and speak up.

Forty Years in the Making

Before moving forward, we need to look back. We gain perspective by doing so. By the time we come to our particular story, Israel has come a long, long way. After being rescued from their four-hundred-year enslavement to Egypt, the people of God are off to the Promised Land—a divinely promised, good land flowing with milk and honey. They have escaped the torturous labor and soul-shredding degradation of slavery to Pharaoh in Egypt.

They have only taken a few steps in their freedom march when they hear the pounding of hooves and grinding of wheels behind them. Pharaoh is pursuing with all his might and deadly resources. He is the lord of the land and will not be defied by slaves. Yet, with their own eyes, they watch Pharaoh's horses and chariots vanish beneath the weight and waves of God's judgment in the Red Sea. God is the Lord, and there is no other.

It was then that the prophet Miriam, and the great company of women in Israel, took up their tambourines singing, "Sing to the Lord, for he has triumphed gloriously; the horse and his rider he has thrown into the sea."[3] If you listen closely, you can still hear the sound as they get their first taste of freedom from tyranny.

From the Red Sea, they journey to Mount Sinai to meet with God and learn how to live this new life as free people under His blessing and in community with one another. From Sinai, they journey through the wilderness accompanied by divine presence, eating the miraculous provision of manna and drinking water from the rock.

After all they've witnessed and experienced, fear and discontentment still eat away at their trust in God. In story after story, the Bible describes a people who complain at every turn, oppose Moses time and again, and finally, as if that isn't enough, come to the very edge of the Promised Land and then . . . *they won't go in.* As a result, the revival movement that began with a miraculous deliverance from Egypt seems to have irreparably fallen apart.

I suppose it wasn't all their fault; there was a bad report. Twelve spies went into the Promised Land to see what would be required of them to settle there. The Lord had given them the land, but they knew they would have to fight to take possession. Long before the spies were sent, there had been a census, a counting, of all the men old enough and capable of going to war.[4] Girls weren't counted in that census because it was for military purposes. Now everyone was awaiting the reconnaissance report, anxious to hear about their new land and hoping it would be an easy undertaking for fear of losing husbands, fathers, brothers, and sons.

The spies tell the good news first. The land was just as God had said! It flowed with milk and honey, a fruitful and fertile land capable of yielding good crops, feeding livestock, and sustaining an entire nation. The people rejoice, perhaps dance a little, and slap each other on the back. The women, perhaps, began reaching for their tambourines, preparing to sing another song, or perhaps they began gathering the children and packing their belongings.

Then came the bad news—the report God called *evil*: It's a good land, but we can't have it. They said, "We are not able to go up against the people, for they are stronger than we are."[5] At this news, the people throw away their confidence in God. They fall into unbelief. Their rejoicing turns to fear, their grumbling produces rebellion, and they accuse God of leading them, their wives, and their children into the wilderness to die. "And they said to one another, 'Let us choose a leader and go back to Egypt.'"[6]

Their unbelief and sin result in exile from the good land flowing with milk and honey, reminding us of a scene in Eden when Adam and Eve rebelled by believing the word of a serpent over the word of God. As a result, an entire generation is turned away and sent back into the wilderness to wander until another generation can arise. But lest we think God heartless, in His mercy and kindness, the Promised Land is kept for them—passed on to the new generation.

This is where our story begins—forty years later—where one generation's journey failed and a new generation's journey is about to start, at the threshold of the Promised Land.

A New Count

Forty years later, everything is different, but nothing has changed. The land has been given but has yet to be taken. God did not change His mind, though the last generation had. He had given the land, and it was still given; His promises never fail. The tribes are gathered for the preparation and reorganization for entry. It is a new time and generation, but the Promised Land still has its giants, and taking possession will still be a fight. The ones who'd been numbered decades earlier, the men capable of going to war, were all gone. A new count was needed.

So, sons twenty years old and upward were numbered according to their father's house. They totaled a staggering 601,730.[7] We are told the census is, once again, to discover the size and strength of their armed forces. Indeed, before a new census had been decided upon, there had been trouble predetermining war. What's more, in very short order, the battle of Jericho would mark the inauguration of the taking of the land given by God. But, still, war is not the only reason for a new census. There is also the matter of the land that had been *promised*.

Hebrews tells us that by faith Abraham left everything he had known, including his country, kindred, and immediate family to obey the call of God. He did this without knowing the exact directions, to "go out to a place that he was to receive as an inheritance."[8] God promised to give Abraham land as a divine inheritance, a land that would support his family (as many as the sands of the sea or stars in the sky) so they could flourish and bless all the families of the earth.

From that time, as the descendants of Abraham grew into multitudes of people (the twelve tribes of Israel), they had been looking for a home, a land of their own, a place where they would settle. So, for generations they had lived as nomads, picking up and putting down tents as they moved again and again and again.

When famine came, they moved to Egypt and were favored by Pharaoh for Joseph's sake until Joseph and that Pharaoh died. Then, for generations, they lived as enslaved people in a country not their own until the great exodus, when Moses led them out on their present journey to the Promised Land. This was a land where they might be free to live and worship their God. The land that would support their future hopes. The land where they could finally settle in, feel a sense of belonging, and call home. The land they could cultivate and pass on as an inheritance for their children and their children's children.

From the time I was sixteen, I wanted a home and a family. When Mike and I were first married, we lacked the financial resources to buy our own home. For us, renting with children in tow was hard. Each time I became pregnant, we were told we were over the limit (of children) for our lease. Having children should not be a reason for eviction! In the first eight years of our marriage, we moved ten times. It was exhausting.

I longed to have a home to call my own. I wanted to hang curtains and wallpaper, paint rooms whatever colors I'd fancy, arrange furniture, plant trees in the backyard, and place potted plants in the front. I longed for my children to feel established and secure, able to cultivate friendships without the fear of leaving too soon and cutting those relationships short. When we bought our first home, I turned to Mike and said, "I don't want to move again for at least five years." We did not move for 33. Our children played in the streets of our neighborhood, and so did their children. Those were good years filled with many treasured memories.

The promise of land given by God to His people, however, meant even more than realizing the longing for home and family. It was an enactment of fulfilling the original mandate given in the Garden. God created the heavens and the earth to sustain life, for He is a life-giving and life-preserving God. The mandate in the Garden was for human beings to bring all of creation into flourishing by caring for creation and all that's in it and caring for our families and neighbors the way God has cared for us. Evil makes the land suffer; righteousness gives the land life so that the trees clap their hands and the calves dance.

The inheritance of land is the tangible, physical manifestation of God's spiritual blessing and calling, giving His people the means to possess and fulfill what they were born for as those made in His image. The physical and the spiritual are not at odds. The physical is meant to be spiritualized, and the spiritual is meant to be materialized. God and His promises are real.

Now the census begins. House by father's house, tribe by tribe, the sons are counted, starting with the tribe of Reuben. Verse after verse, the counting drones on; the sons of Reuben and their clans, the sons of Simeon and their clans, the sons of Gad and their clans, the sons of Judah, of Issachar, of Zebulun, and Joseph and their clans. Then, suddenly, we are interrupted by a note that seems as entirely out of place as a horse in a sequined ball gown.

"Now Zelophehad the son of Hepher had no sons, but daughters. And the names of the daughters of Zelophehad were Mahlah, Noah, Hoglah, Milcah, and Tirzah."[9] No explanation is given at all, just two short sentences about some poor guy without any sons. Then, just as suddenly, the naming of tribes, clans, and sons resumes. The sons of Ephraim and their clans, the sons of Benjamin and their clans, the sons of Dan and their clans, etc. It seems to make no sense at all.

In a book where sons are the ones who count, why not simply say he had no sons and leave it at that? Perhaps sons are not the only ones who count, after all. Perhaps the Lord wants His daughters to see something beyond the obvious. Remember, the census counted 601,730 sons. Of those, only six are not clan leaders. They are daughters. Asher had sons and a daughter named Serah, who is not heard from again or in our story, so she remains a bit of a mystery (like all of us). The other five daughters are sisters. They are the daughters of Zelophehad, who had no sons. The author is intentional here, drawing our attention to something easily overlooked, but something that would change history.

It's the Law

> The LORD spoke to Moses, saying, "Among these the land shall be divided for inheritance according to the number of names. . . . According to the names of the tribes of their fathers they shall inherit. Their inheritance shall be divided according to lot between the larger and the smaller."[10]

As soon as the new count is complete, we find out how the land will be divided. Each family will get a share, an inheritance in the form of land, and each share will be apportioned according to the size of the clan and the number of sons, or more precisely, according to the tribes of their fathers.

This is important. A good father leaves an inheritance to his sons so that the family line is preserved, and the name of the tribal clan continues. Lineage is important. The names preserve the identification of the seed line; the covenant family line began with Adam and followed along to Abraham, Isaac, and Jacob, and then on to Joseph, King David, and so on until the coming of Mary, Joseph, and finally Jesus, the Messiah, the Seed. The prophecy spoken in the Garden of Eden about the seed of the woman who will crush the head of the serpent comes to fulfillment because it is true, and it is real. It materializes through the seed line divinely preserved and protected from generation to generation according to the names of the tribes of the fathers and their sons until Jesus—the son of David, the son of Abraham—is revealed.[11]

Sons, therefore, inherit the land. If a father has no sons, the inheritance is to be given to his brothers. One man, Zelophehad, had no sons. He had five daughters. The inheritance—*the Promised Land*—was to be given to another man's son. Among his tribe and clan, Zelophehad's name would cease to exist. This is just not right.

A New Chapter

> Then drew near the daughters of Zelophehad. . . . And they stood before Moses and before Eleazar the priest and before the chiefs and all the congregation, at the entrance of the tent of meeting, saying. . . . "Give to us a possession among our father's brothers."[12]

A few short verses ago, we had a seemingly incongruent notation about five daughters. Now those daughters draw near to the elders. Not only is this a new chapter, but it is also an unprecedented request, a new request from a new generation for a new time. As is true so often, when women are introduced into the situation, something is about to be changed, shifted, and re-directed in a new trajectory.

Together as a family unit, they draw near under the name of their father, Zelophehad. All females, yes, but still a family clan. They came to the tent of meeting, where Moses would meet with God. Only the most essential matters were brought before Moses to be decided by divine arbitration. The tent of meeting is where judgments and rulings for the nation were decided. It was a type of supreme court. Together the daughters came and stood, in full view of the entire community, before the highest-ranking leaders of the nation, including Moses the prophet, Eleazer the priest, all the chieftains, and all the recently counted men.

They are incredibly bold. I wonder where they learned such courage. Did they find their strength in their numbers? The number five in Scripture connotes grace.[13] Perhaps being a company of five emboldened and enabled them. Wisdom tells us that two are better than one because we accomplish more, encourage and assist one another, and can effectively stand against opposition.[14] The sisters had each other.

Did they learn courage from their parents? No mother is mentioned, so I look to their father, Zelophehad, who had no sons. Did he pine for sons or treasure his daughters? Did he see his girls' value, strength, and tenacity? Did he tell them they could be brave like Sarah, Leah, Rachel, Rebekah, Tamar, Jochebed, and Miriam as he recounted their stories and their *me-od*? He must have, I imagine, for his daughters are undoubtedly courageous, and a father who loves and encourages his daughters to rise to the fullness of the call on their lives—without apology or playing small—is one of the most formidable and transformative influences in a girl's life.

Scripture is eager to point out that our heavenly Father does precisely this for His daughters, whom He loves, so it is not hard to imagine. So, likewise, Scripture allows us to envision Zelophehad doing the same for his.

These courageous daughters decide to speak up without precedent or guarantee of the outcome. They ask to be counted among the sons of every clan, placed on equal footing with their father's brothers, that they might receive the inheritance through their father. They were asking for a change in the law, which would require an answer from God Himself for reformation. It was an incredibly bold move, not because it was against the rules, but because *it wasn't in the rules.*

This was not a question of provision. Fathers commonly provided daughters with a dowry upon marriage. The dowry included household items and other valuables, and often even a servant or two. In this way, the daughters received a type of inheritance from their parents.[15] The question was not about provision. Instead, the question was whether daughters—girls—were suitable heirs of their fathers.

Why do the daughters care? Why does Scripture care enough to take up half a chapter highlighting this story? To find the answer, we must broaden our examination and look at their bravery in the context of the prior few chapters. In them, we see contrast and comparison alluding to something more—*much* more. Remember, a new generation of Israel is making its way toward the land God has promised them as an inheritance.

The surrounding nations know that a multitude of people, who are called Israel, has arrived at their doorstep, having camped in the plains of Moab near Jericho. They had seen "all that Israel had done to the Amorites."[16] The leaders and the nations of Moab and Midian are terrified. Balak, the king of Moab, hires a prophet (whom Scripture later labels false because he led the people astray to idols for personal gain) named Balaam to come and curse Israel. Fortunately for Israel, Balaam is constrained by God and can only bless and not curse Israel.[17]

The scheme to curse Israel has failed, and a new scheme has been invented. Foreign women are sent among the Israelite people to lead the men into idolatry. This scheme works, and the men begin worshiping false gods, bringing the judgment of God upon them. Even as Moses is attempting to put the seduction of his people to death, an Israelite chieftain brings Cozbi, the daughter of a Midianite chieftain, to the tent of meeting in a scandalous display of harlotry.[18]

On the eve of possessing the promise, after experiencing the rebellion of the last generation, which sentenced a generation to death in the wilderness, a new generation is now being seduced to the same end. The instrument of destruction? Women. Daughters of foreign clan leaders (fathers) who serve other gods and seduce men to keep them from their inheritance. Don't miss seeing that the place it culminates is the entrance to the tent of meeting in full sight of Moses the prophet and the entire congregation. These women, unlike Zelophehad's daughters, are used by men for their own purposes. They are abused and abusive, false even to themselves as they are part of making these Israelites false to their God. And all that wickedness culminates in the shadow of the presence of God in the tent of meeting.

The zeal of the son of Aaron, the priest, ended the tragedy. You see, there was still a man of faith in Israel. What's more, there were daughters of chieftains in Israel who were righteous and faithful before God—the daughters of Zelophehad. These women would stand at the entrance of the tent of meeting to preserve the inheritance of the fathers.

Going back just a little further, we read the story of the five sisters in the context of the spies who bring an evil report discouraging the people from believing that the good land given by God can be taken. The people, the spies (except for Joshua and Caleb), fail in their faith and ask for a new leader to be appointed to take them back to Egypt. They did not believe they would receive the land promised.

Astoundingly, the Hebrew word for "appointed" in the above verse is the same word used by the five sisters when they ask for their father's inheritance.[19] Unlike the former generation, but like Joshua and Caleb, the sisters believed in God's promise. They believed they would come into and possess the Promised Land. They already loved the land, and it was a catalyst for their muchness.

Embedded in the original language of our story, the Holy Spirit is using words to convey that this is what faith looks like. It looks like opening our hearts wide with love for what God—who, out of love, gives—has promised to give us before it has materialized. Isn't this what we realize from the lives of those in the hall of faith when we read about the extraordinary obedience of ordinary men and women who acted on God's word without knowing the outcome, hoping beyond the present, believing into the future?[20]

Speak Up and Speak Right

All eyes are on the sisters who have drawn near. With one voice, they state their case humbly, transparently, without self-pity or bitter complaint. They tell the truth without minimization, manipulation, or accusation.

> "Our father died in the wilderness. He was not among the company of those who gathered themselves together against the LORD

in the company of Korah, but died for his own sin. And he had no sons. Why should the name of our father be taken away from his clan because he had no son? Give to us a possession among our father's brothers."[21]

They affirm God's judgment against such sinful rebellion as displayed by the company of Korah, for which the earth opened up, utterly consuming them, erasing their name and posterity among the tribes of Israel. They ceased to exist. They would not receive any inheritance of the promises of God in the land. This is right in their eyes. Their father, they acknowledge, died for his own sin. Still, they refuse to allow his name to be dishonored, swallowed up, and forever lost for being wrongfully associated or having offspring of the wrong gender.

They appeal to the elders for an inheritance in the land to preserve their father's house. They clearly desire to preserve the past and ensure the future of the family line. It was a bold appeal. Now they wait for an answer. They have yet to learn how their request will be received and perceived. All they can do is wait and see.

At times, in some religious settings, strong women who dare to speak up have been misunderstood. In my years of serving as a leader in the Body of Christ, I have encountered this. I have been called names, been sent letters of rebuke, and more. Unfortunately, like many of my colleagues, I have found it not uncommon to be labeled a "Jezebel." This is not only unfortunate, but it is also wrong. Deeply wrong. There is a boldness that is also righteous, holy, born of the spirit of the prophets.

The sisters have modeled this for us. Jezebel, in contrast, was brazen and unrighteous. She was a queen who lived in the time of Elijah, the prophet.[22] She was known for leading the people of God into idolatrous practices and for murdering prophets.

Jezebel cared nothing about preserving a family's inheritance or namesake, unlike the daughters of Zelophehad.

When her husband pouted over a plot of land belonging to an Israelite man named Naboth, she falsely accused him of sin, knowing he would be stoned to death. His supposed sin and subsequent death allowed her to confiscate his promised land, a gift from God to preserve his name, his tribe, and his family line. She manipulated the system and agreed with the accuser of the brethren for personal gain. No, Jezebel is nothing like the daughters of Zelophehad. And being a strong, female leader with humble boldness of speech is nothing like being Jezebel.

The five sisters—the daughters of Zelophehad—were *me-od*. And they were right to be so. The greatest danger in front of the daughters, however, was settling for the status quo and a watered-down version of what God had promised. I heard someone once say that sometimes when we add up all we are up against—the challenges, the work, the heartbreak, and the evil—we may as well play it small and settle. This, however, is not the way of the God of Scripture, who never settles for less than His best for us and all of creation. He never settles for the status quo of society, culture, or systems that have forgotten the way of righteousness, justice, and mercy. What God desires for us, and for our neighbors, is always better than what we desire for ourselves.

This story highlights a different way forward by introducing a request made by women to change a system in which men couldn't see the need for change. The sisters, like their God, refused to settle for less than justice on behalf of their gender, their father, and the generations to come. By their boldness to make this request, they pioneered a new way forward for a new generation entering a new land.

Moses takes the issue before God without assuming to know the answer, but knowing that without divine decree, the laws could not be changed. God speaks.

> "The daughters of Zelophehad are right. You shall give them possession of an inheritance among their father's brothers. . . . 'If a man dies and has no son, then you shall transfer his inheritance to his daughter. . . . And it shall be for the people of Israel a statute and rule, as the LORD commanded Moses.'"[23]

And just like that, the inheritance laws of Israel are forever changed. This case in Hebrew history has been named the oldest case still cited as an authority in law courts today. In fact, in 1924, the American Bar upheld women's inheritance rights standing on this ancient Jewish law, which the daughters of Zelophehad had established.[24]

Think of it! The courage and cunning of the daughters of Zelophehad would affect a nation of women not yet in existence and hundreds of years in the future. They could never have seen nor imagined it. Yet God, the God who is able to do so much more than we could ever ask, think, or imagine,[25] not only saw it, but He intended it. He saw faith in those sisters that would move mountains far into the future, and He meant for those mountains to be removed. He meant for us to see what He could do with a woman who was full of faith and willing to risk finding her voice before the great, the influential, and the powerful in any and every human system.

The daughters of Zelophehad pioneered the way for generations to come in their nation. The day they stepped forward to take a stand and speak up, they honored their father, secured the future for their children, and changed the world for other women. And not just other women in Israel. In response to their faith in God's promises, their righteous request, and their love for the land—in response to their *muchness*—God issued a new statute that would be for every new generation.

Find Your *Me-od* Voice

"I'm not asking much. Just a token really, a trifle. You'll never even miss it. What I want from you is your voice," the sea witch beguiled.[26] To be human is to have a voice because our God is a speaking God. He spoke all things into existence and upholds the universe by the power of His word.[27] More than simply saying words, to have a voice is to have a responsibility. Words have power and carry authority. With them, we offer God our thanksgiving and adoration. To others, we convey a sense of who we are and who God is. With our words, we create ideas and express emotion. We communicate, collaborate, give permission, and set boundaries. And so much more. Diane Langberg explains, "The God who is called the Word intends for those created in his image to have a voice. . . . He created us to speak. He does not want that voice silenced or crushed."[28]

Since we are made in the image of God, our voices are to reflect the nature of God, speaking up not only on behalf of ourselves and our interests, but also on behalf of those whose voices have been silenced or crushed under the weight of oppression, injustice, victimization, sin, demonic bondage, fear, and intimidation. The voiceless have lost the freedom to express their needs, desires, and pain. When they do speak, they are too often not heard. Our God is the God of the voiceless. He sent His Son, the Word, to speak on behalf of those who cannot speak. And He wants to speak through us on their behalf.

Finding your voice, then, means having the courage and the cunning—the *muchness*—to speak up in relationships and in conversations to express your insight, understanding, and viewpoint on matters that matter to God, to you, and to those around you. It means allowing your heart to be broken by what breaks the heart of God, giving way to the groaning of the Spirit over what is just not right until words are divinely formed and informed, becoming righteous speech.

It means refusing to allow intimidation or the threat of loss to render us silent. It means seizing the opportunity to change the rules and gain the fullness of the inheritance God has for us and for the generations of women coming behind us. The daughters of Zelophehad found their *muchness*. Now we must find ours!

They found it in part by listening. Unlike anyone else in the book of Numbers, they understand how to speak boldly without dishonoring or being rebellious. They could face Moses without facing off with him. They could speak up without speaking against his leadership. They could call for change without calling down the judgment of God on anyone. They were not only courageous, but they were also cunning, discerning, and wise. And that kind of wisdom comes only by careful observation and by listening to the still, small voice.

Your voice may have been silenced or crushed. May our Lord Jesus come to you even as you read these words to comfort your heart, heal your pain and trauma, and redeem and restore all that is lost. If all you can do right now is sit in the dirt like Job, I sit with you as your friend, weep with you, and mourn your losses. And I pray for the day when your mourning is turned to dancing, and the pain you have suffered becomes a cry of justice and deliverance for others.

Until then, know that your voice is kept for you in the hand of mighty God, and may the God of all comfort, through the Lord Jesus Christ and in the power of the Spirit, comfort you and give you peace. If you listen, and keep listening, to the still, small voice, you'll find your own voice—in all of its strength and power.

4

Dare to Lead!

THE STORY OF TWO LEADERS

· JUDGES 4–5 ·

"For the LORD will deliver Sisera into *the hands of a woman.*"[1]

*W*E CAN DO IT!" You've seen her many times: the iconic wartime Rosie the Riveter with her arm raised, flexing her muscles. She was only a cartoon, an artistic rendering, but she called out to an untapped power source that was living on every street and neighborhood in America. She called out to an undercover army that would trade in their silk stockings for overalls, uniforms, hammers, and guns. She offered an opportunity to break with every cultural limitation and expectation of what it meant to be female to stand in the workplace and on the battlefield in occupations and callings once only filled by men. She called on women to offer their powerful minds and muscles to help turn the tide of war. She called. They answered.

According to the United States Department of Defense, approximately five million civilian women joined the war effort during WWII, working as riveters, masons, welders, and more. About 350,000 served in uniform. Some were killed by enemy fire, others were captured and held prisoner, a few thousand received medals for bravery or combat, and still others were sent to Normandy just days after the intense and brutal invasion.[2]

There is a quotation carved into the cement blocks of the World War II memorial in Washington, D.C., that reads, "Women who stepped up were measured as citizens of the nation, not as women. This was a people's war and everyone was in it."[3] The pressures of WWII erased at least some of the limits of gender in America for a time, allowing women to discover and reveal their strength.

It took a world war to reveal to a great majority in America something that Scripture has been proclaiming all along: Women are powerful. Women are a grace, a wonder of God. Women are intelligent, skillful, and shrewd. Women are called, commissioned, gifted, and raised to do great and mighty things. Regarding the cosmic war we are in, God measures women as citizens of the Kingdom, not as women. The culture may be confused about what a woman is, but God is not. And we, as the women of God, should not be.

Like a Girl

The inception of cultural limitations and expectations placed on women is not found in 21st-century America. It begins with a snake in a Garden; however, the Garden story is long, so let's not start there. Let's start with a startling story about another vulnerable time in a woman's life: puberty.

The company Always, which produces feminine pads, began losing impact and influence among 16- to 24-year-olds. As they started their research into the life of girls during puberty, they had no idea the staggering fact they would uncover. They discovered that girls go through a crisis of confidence at that time. The study showed that a girl's self-esteem drops twice as much as a boy's during puberty and never returns to pre-puberty levels when she becomes a woman.

> Gender stereotypes have a big impact on girls during puberty, as this is the time when they learn what it means to be a girl, and young womanhood comes to be defined by a set of rules, like beauty and submissiveness. Society constantly dwells on gender differences, sending out the message that leadership, power, and strength are for men, not for women. . . . These stereotypes inevitably crystallize into girls' self-perceptions and affect their behaviours.[4]

Always wanted to test this conclusion, so they conducted a social experiment. They held a fake casting call with young women, men, boys, and girls asking them to run, fight, and more, using the descriptor "like a girl." The women, boys, and men behaved in a "silly and self-deprecating way, acting out the insulting stereotype."

The prepubescent girls, however, ran and fought daringly with confidence. Not having yet been influenced by the culture, they thought "doing something 'like a girl' meant doing it as best as they could."[5] Indeed, it does, and so much more. Society is not the only one with something to say about what it means to do something *like a girl*. It is not even the important one.

The message of Scripture will restore and revive the confidence, callings, and dreams of women everywhere. We will run, fight, and even lead when we hear that message. We will do it with boldness, permanently breaking out of the restraints placed on what women can do, inside and outside the Church, and our God is cheering us on to do it all *like a girl*.

Follow the Leader

History shows us that God has called and raised women at the forefront of every revival movement. Women see what's missing and create new ways to bring solutions, healing, and prosperity to families, cities, and nations. Throughout history, women have been abolitionists, social entrepreneurs and activists, revivalists, missionaries, and revolutionaries. They have been apostles, prophets, evangelists, pastors, and teachers written about in Scripture, in the early Church, and throughout Church history.

In Scripture, God raises up women as heroes and leaders to bring a shift in challenging circumstances. Their role is essential for changing the course of events, preserving the community's well-being, and safeguarding the perpetuation of God's agenda and prophetic promises. God hears the cry of the oppressed and suffering, and He appoints women, just as He does men, to be His instruments of salvation and deliverance.

Rahab's shrewdness helped fell Jericho,[6] Esther's political savvy prevented a holocaust,[7] the unnamed wise woman's clever negotiations ended a murderous rampage,[8] much as Abigail did,[9] and Deborah and Jael's daring leadership ended a tyrannical reign of terror.[10] The story of these two women, Deborah and Jael, needs a fresh hearing.

Village Life Had Ceased

Our story begins in a time of cruel oppression, depression, economic insecurity, fear, and suffering. It was the time of the judges, a time of severe moral decline, when the people of God were turning away from Him to worship the gods of other nations. God had warned them about the seduction they would face if they mixed in marriage, commerce, and life with those who did not know Him. He had also warned them about the consequences of suffering it would invite into their lives, individually and corporately.

The people didn't listen, and the consequences were disastrous. The highways were abandoned, travelers kept to the byways, and village life had ceased.[11] This is a poetic way of saying business and trade could not be conducted, and villagers and their families were not safe in their towns because of the dangerous, corrupt, crime-ridden culture. Further, for twenty years, the people had suffered and lived in fear of a great oppressor, Jabin, king of Canaan, whose reign of terror by iron chariot forbade their deliverance and sealed their torment.

The situation was hopeless, which is the point at which God's work can begin. In each historical narrative in the book of Judges, deliverance requires divine intervention. And that intervention begins at the point of human failure and limitation. When nothing is left but the cry for God, God finds the room He needs to act. Each time, we read of our faithful God responding to the cry of His suffering people by raising up a deliverer who will defeat the enemy, leading the way back to Him and into freedom.

In this story where there are nine hundred chariots of iron in a region where it is too dangerous to walk the streets, we are being set up to expect a deliverer such as Samson, perhaps another Moses, or better still, Joshua. We are being set up to be taken off guard when God does the unexpected. God doesn't raise up a man at all. He raises up two women. We are to be stunned, taken aback, and shaken awake. We are to be moved out of old paradigms and traditions and understand that God will appoint and anoint whomever He chooses, regardless of any limitation placed upon them by cultural, religious, or societal norms.

Dare to Lead

Leadership, like heroism, is genderless. Leadership is based on gifting and calling. And gifting and calling come from God—as He wills. As women, we are measured as citizens of the Kingdom of God, not according to gender or marital status, but according to our personal integrity before God. We all need to understand what the Bible says about women in leadership and ministry. I write about this critical theology in chapter 8. For now, notice that as we move forward in our story, God explains His theology of women in leadership by calling one woman to the highest place of leadership in the nation and by crediting another with decisively defeating the enemy on behalf of the country.

Calling and gifting come from the Lord alone. The culture does not dictate them. Even in our story, the reader is meant to be shocked by whom the Lord calls and anoints. Anointing and gifting come from the Holy Spirit. The promise of the pouring out of the Holy Spirit, prophesied by Joel, Isaiah, and Jeremiah, came without gender specification.

When the Day of Pentecost arrived, the Holy Spirit was poured out on the 120 in the Upper Room, both male and female. Each is considered a disciple of Jesus, now anointed by the Spirit, given gifts to live a life of obedience to every word that comes from the mouth of God and serve Christ in the lives of others.[12]

The apostle Paul grounds the spiritual gifts and the calling of God in the Holy Spirit and never once distinguishes between gifts and callings for male versus female.[13] Again, the author of Hebrews tells us the Holy Spirit distributes His gifts according to His own will and desire, not according to sex, education, social status, ethnicity, age, or wealth.[14]

Did you know that every person has a sphere of leadership? Wherever you have authority and influence, in a place or circumstance or with a people group, is your sphere of leadership. It is in your sphere of leadership that you have a responsibility to lead.

Meet Deborah at Her Palm Tree

Deborah, a prophetess, the wife of Lappidoth, was judging Israel at that time. She used to sit under the palm of Deborah between Ramah and Bethel. . . . and the people of Israel came up to her for judgment.[15]

Deborah is introduced with scant, but illuminating, detail. Meet Deborah: prophet, wife of Lappidoth, and judge of the nation of Israel.[16] The mention of being the wife of Lappidoth, in between her calling as a prophet and her role as judge, is curious. The Hebrew here, "לַפִּידוֹת אֵשֶׁת (*lappidoth esheth*)," can be translated as "wife of Lappidoth," or more literally, "woman of torches." Again, curiously, we find Lappidoth in no other place in all of Scripture. We cannot, therefore, discover his family line, the tribe to which he belongs, the city in which he originates, his position, work, or role. These are the common identifiers for men of Israel. It seems likely that the literal rendering, "woman of torches," comes nearer to capturing the truth of Deborah's identity.

Susan Niditch and others argue for the translation "woman of torches," suggesting that Deborah is presented as a charismatic leader—not a "domesticated version of the woman warrior" (Niditch, Judges, 62, 65; Ackerman, Warrior, Dancer, Seductress, Queen, 38). The designation "woman of torches" would then mean something like "fiery woman" (Ackerman, Warrior, 38). . . . Since Deborah fills the role of prophet and judge throughout Judg 4–5, it would be surprising for her to be introduced in the role of wife (O'Connor, "The Women in the Book of Judges," 279–80).[17]

Even if *wife* of Lappidoth is the correct translation, although it seems unlikely, the role is mentioned second to her role as a prophet, and her husband is neither heard from nor about from this point on. He is not significant to or the focus of the plot (although, if he existed, he would be important to God). The point of the matter is, he is *not* the leader. He is not the one appointed and anointed to effect deliverance for the nation. Deborah *is*. She is God's answer to the cry of His people.

I am often asked if a woman can lead if her husband is not called to lead alongside her. The answer, clearly, is yes. Deborah is our example. Whether married, single, male, or female, each is individually responsible to answer the call of God. This does not negate the responsibility of both men and women, husbands and wives, and male and female leaders to stand alongside one another, submit to and prefer one another, love one another, and remain faithful in covenant, in community to one another and to God. If God is calling you to lead, dare to lead!

Deborah is the first prophet leader-deliverer over the nation of Israel since the great prophet Moses. She takes her place in the line of his succession. Like priests and kings, the anointing of the Holy Spirit was upon her in a special way to be empowered to lead and speak for God to His people. This was no small matter, as she would be representing God, speaking for God, and executing God's divine will, just as Moses had done. Her anointed role, therefore, was governance. She was responsible for the oversight, care, and protection of God's people—children, women, and men.

Day after day, Deborah sat under the palm tree, the symbol of justice, where she administered counsel and rendered decisions in legal matters. The place where she sat, the geography where her palm tree was planted, symbolized her judicial authority planted over the entire nation, rooted in divine authority and holding sway over the "sons of Israel," the male tribal leaders who *came up* to come under her judgments.

> In the ancient world, the legislative and executive aspects of ruling were bound together with, and indeed often derived from, the judicial role of the king or leader. This connection may be seen from the biblical descriptions of the 'judges' who act on God's behalf in Israel (e.g. Judg. 2:16–18; 4:4–10). Kings in Israel, like the judges before them, were to mediate God's rule in the world, 'to effect just judgment and righteousness' (āśāh mišpāṭ ûṣeḏāqâ; 2 Sam. 8:15; Jer. 22:3; Ps. 72:1–4; cf. Isa. 9:6).[18]

In the time when judges ruled, Deborah was called by God as a judge. God saw fit to call and commission her to be the leader of a nation, trusting her with the responsibility of carrying out His mandates and His word.

She moved in the power of the Spirit, filled with the fire of God. And her story urges us to remember our own calling, to take up our torches—to prophesy, to judge, to lead, to rule. God has set the standard for what He will call a woman to do.

Meet Jael at Her Tent

"Most blessed of women is Jael, the wife of Heber the Kenite; most blessed is she of women in the tent."

Judges 5:24 NASB

Jael enters the story almost as an "extra" in a movie, just passing by as background texture. We have already been introduced to the situation and all the major players: Judge Deborah; her timid general, Barak; tyrannical King Jabin; and his wicked general, Sisera. Deborah has prophesied the defeat of Jabin and the deliverance of Israel. That credit for deliverance will be given to a woman because of Barak's reluctant response. Then we meet Jael. She is a wife and lives in a tent as part of a nomadic tribe.

When the battle turns against him, the murderous general Sisera flees for cover—not into Deborah's hands, but into Jael's tent. Jael is a homemaker. She has authority and influence in her own home. Her tent is her sphere of leadership, the place she has jurisdiction and renders judgment. Cunningly, without a hint of fear or insecurity, she welcomes him with comforting words and reassures him with motherly hospitality. She gives him a little milk to drink, a blanket to warm and hide him, and a place to rest his head. Sisera and the readers both think he has found safety. After all, there is a "peace" between the evil king and Jael's husband.[19] Thus far, Jael's tribe has remained neutral in Israel's war. Sometimes, peace is only the calm before the storm.

Jael, like all nomadic women, would be skilled in efficiently erecting and discharging her portable dwelling. After years of practice, like David with his sling, a tent peg and hammer are at home in her hands. In a twist of sovereignty, the enemy of all Israel was drifting off to sleep in her tent, having commanded her watch at the door in case any man should come to threaten, oblivious that the real threat was female. In the twinkling of an eye and with the skill of a seasoned warrior, Jael wields her hammer and drives a tent peg through his head.

In one sudden and surprising moment, Deborah's prophecy is fulfilled. The Lord gave the enemy into the hand of a woman. As then, so now. Wake up! God is using women to advance His Kingdom. Leadership is genderless. It is the Lord's doing. Shocking, perhaps, and unexpected by some. Certainly it is untraditional in some circles. But God is the God who turns the world upside down. Our cultural standards and expectations are no barrier to His will.

So, be bold. Let your confidence be unadulterated. Dare to take the lead! You have permission and precedent. God is with you. God is *within* you.

Lead with the Gifts You Have Been Given

Deborah and Jael both aligned with God and were used by Him to further His plan of salvation. They both dared to lead in their spheres of influence. Nevertheless, that is where their similarities end.

Deborah led the nation as prophet and judge with wisdom, knowledge, prophetic insight, oversight, and foresight. She rose as a mother in Israel, commanding an army to resist an oppressor. Jael led in her tent as a homemaker with shrewdness, discernment, and bold action. She rose as a mother in her household, deceiving and defeating the enemy oppressors' military general.

They were two very different women with different histories, geographies, and lifestyles. They both had their calling, gifting, and assignment from God. Their spheres of leadership were also their own, divinely tailored to the call on their lives.

What is your calling? What are your gifts? Where do you already have influence and authority? Where do you have favor with people who trust your decisions and welcome your leadership? Wherever you are in your discovery process, trust that God is positioning you in the proper sphere of leadership wherever you find yourself.

Trust yourself, too. Dare to be yourself at all times, true to who you are with all your history, personality, and uniqueness. This is not to say stop growing and healing and becoming. If you need to take a break from social media—or give it up completely to heal from FOMO (fear of missing out)—or stop living under the pressure to perform while pretending to be someone and something you are not, do it. Do it today. Do it right now.

It means that when you are invited to the table with those you admire and respect, respect and admire yourself as God's image bearer and hold your own, offering your unique opinion, thoughts, and ideas without conforming to social pressure or popular opinion. Be yourself.

Do what you were created to do. You can't do everything. The old commercial hailing women as those who can "bring home the bacon, fry it up in a pan,"[20] suggesting we can do everything all at once, was wrong—to the detriment of a generation of exhausted women. Learn to set boundaries around your schedule, relationships, and emotions. How many burned-out leaders do you know? I know more than I can count. They never learned to set boundaries.

What if you don't yet know to what you are called? Here is my best advice. In response to what moves both the heart of God and your own, use what is already in your hand. What skills, talents, and gifts are already developed in your life? What are you passionate about that the Lord also cares about, as revealed in Scripture?

Harriet Beecher Stowe was the author of *Uncle Tom's Cabin*, an influential book exposing the dark side of slavery during the Civil War. Harriet's sister-in-law urged her to use what God had already put in her hands—the gift to write. "Hattie, if I could use a pen as you can, I would write something that would make this whole nation feel what an accursed thing slavery is." Harriet later said, "I wrote what I did because as a woman, as a mother I was oppressed and brokenhearted, with the sorrows and injustice I saw, because as a Christian I felt the dishonor to Christianity— because as a lover of my country I trembled at the coming day of wrath."[21]

Lead Like a Girl

In my generation (I am now a grandmother of six and counting), one of the things I observed in the marketplace was women leaders trying to lead like men. They took on male characteristics and leadership approaches, to the point of even dressing like them. Before anyone begins to judge, they were trying to fit into a culture that wasn't at ease with women being, well, feminine. For too long, women in leadership have been caught in a "double bind." If she is too soft, she is disrespected, and if she is too strong, she is deemed unlikeable.[22] Things are changing, but we still have a way to go.

Let's not place women in a box to say they should look, dress, or speak in any particular way. Women come in all shapes, sizes, processing styles, and personalities. *Femaleness* cannot be grouped into a neat category, list of outward expressions, or stylistic choices. This is not the point I am trying to make. The point is that we, as girls (or women), bring value to the table. We are not simply counterparts to the men in our lives—our fathers, our brothers, our husbands, our sons. We are friends of God, co-laborers with Christ, warriors in the Spirit.

The Strength of a Woman

There is a reason why I always chuckle at the mention of a "man cold." It isn't because I think men are weak, but rather because when I was a young mom, I seemed to be able to handle my own illness while also caring for the children, finishing the laundry, getting dinner on the table, and completing my office or schoolwork. Don't get me wrong; I was married to a wonderful man who was a strong leader in the face of danger but who trembled in the face of a cold. This, of course, is a gross generalization about the differences between men and women, but it is one of those illustrations that helps clarify where we are headed.

There are many natural abilities that women employ and operate in more often than men (but not exclusively so). Women are relational. The value of being relational means women tend to be natural facilitators, networkers, and collaborators, enhancing the connection and communication within a group or a team. (We talk much more about the value of female collaboration in another chapter, so stay tuned!)

Women are contextual thinkers. Dr. Helen E. Fisher explains the values of this way of thinking she calls "web thinking."

> Women integrate more details faster and arrange these bits of
> data into more complex patterns. As they make decisions, women

tend to weigh more variables, consider more options, and see a wider array of possible solutions . . . women are better able to tolerate ambiguity . . . exercise more intuition . . . plot a long-term course. . . . Women's brain architecture for web thinking has endowed them with another natural talent—mental flexibility . . . an essential trait of leadership in our dynamic global economy.[23]

Women are verbal. Um, yeah. Again, Fisher makes a great point: "Words are women's tools. Words still sway minds and hearts."[24] Some women will never say or write a word, yet their life speaks. When they have no words or cannot speak, women speak with their hearts, their countenances, their deeds, their very presence.

Women are sensitive and aware with a kind of discernment that reads between the lines and perceives when something non-verbal is being communicated. Think of it as a sort of mind-reading ability that comes, according to Fisher, from a women's executive brain function and social skills.[25] A woman's natural talents employed in the home, in the marketplace, and in the church are invaluable.

Several years ago, I happened upon something called "the girl effect." In a book entitled *Half the Sky*, authors Nicolas Kristoff and Sheryl WuDunn report that there is evidence suggesting that investment into the development of women can successfully combat poverty and transform communities.[26] When young girls are given help and education, they put off marriage and child-bearing (girls in impoverished Third World nations commonly have children at the age of thirteen), finish their education, start businesses, and then turn to help their parents, siblings, and communities. Girls add value at every level of leadership and society.

A Mother's Anointing

Let's return to our story of Deborah and Jael. After the victory of Sisera's defeat, Deborah sings a song: "I, Deborah, arose, until I arose, a mother in Israel."[27] In our introduction to her, there is no mention of natural children, yet she identifies herself as a mother. A similar situation occurs when we learn of Jael. There is no mention of children, and yet in the telling of the story, we find her mothering Sisera so much so that he feels safe enough to fall asleep under her protection.

If they were not mothers per se, how do we interpret what is being conveyed? When Deborah arose as a mother in Israel, she was rising with authority, gifting, and the positioning of her heart toward the people God had given into her care. She would give her life to ensure their continuance, well-being, and divine destiny. This is what it looks like to have a mother's heart and anointing.

A mother's heart is a reflection of *God's* heart. In Numbers 11, Moses protests to God, claiming that he is not Israel's mother, implying that God is. Moses knew that God alone can truly conceive and bring forth new life. God alone can truly nurture and raise to maturity. And Isaiah recognized that God's love is even more pure motherly than any human mother can give: "Can a woman forget her nursing child, that she should have no compassion on the son of her womb? Even these may forget, yet I will not forget you."[28] When Paul tells the Thessalonians that he was among them as a nursing mother, or the Galatians that he was in the pains of childbirth again, he was showing the mothering heart of the God we call Father.

Some reject any such talk of God. But Scripture is clear. And the truth is obvious: All good comes from God and is a reflection of the good God is and shares. All the goodness of motherhood is God's, as all the goodness of childhood is. Not every woman is a mother, of course. But every woman—and every man—can and should be motherly as God is motherly.

As I have said many times already, our identity is not in our roles as wife or sister or daughter or mother. Our identity is in our calling from God, which includes those roles but is not limited to them. We do not exist merely to perform social functions. We exist to love and be loved by God and to collaborate with Him in His care for the world.

The Original Mother's Day

Initially, Mother's Day reflected this same principle. In 1870, long before Mother's Day became the sentimental day honoring moms, Julia Howe wrote what is known as the Mother's Day Proclamation as a call for peace and disarmament and for women to unite against war. Her idea was influenced by a young Appalachian homemaker, Anna Jarvis, who organized women throughout the Civil War to work for better sanitary conditions for Union and Confederate communities through what she called Mother's Workdays.[29]

In other words, the original Mother's Day was a call to women to join forces and effect societal change.[30] Here is Howe's Mother's Day proclamation:

> Arise, then, Christian women of this day! Arise, all women who have hearts, whether our baptism be of water or of tears! Say firmly: We will not have great questions decided by irrelevant agencies. Our husbands will not come to us, reeking with carnage, for caresses and applause. Our sons shall not be taken from us

to unlearn all that we have been able to teach them of charity, mercy and patience.[31]

It reminds me of another anthem, "In the days of Shamgar, son of Anath, in the days of Jael, the highways were abandoned, and travelers kept to the byways. The villagers ceased in Israel; they ceased to be until I arose; I, Deborah, arose as a mother in Israel."[32]

The Devil's Ploy

Deborah and Jael are not the only mothers mentioned in the passage of Scripture from whom we learn something valuable.

> Out of the window she peered, the mother of Sisera wailed through the lattice: "Why is his chariot so long in coming? Why tarry the hoofbeats of his chariots?" Her wisest princesses answer, indeed, she answers herself, "Have they not found and divided the spoil?— A womb or two for every man; spoil of dyed materials for Sisera, spoil of dyed materials embroidered, two pieces of dyed work embroidered for the neck as spoil?"[33]

To put it bluntly, Sisera's mother and sisters are sitting around waiting for their hero to return home. When he seems delayed, they comfort themselves by calmly commenting he and his men are probably just enjoying sexually assaulting the women. They are not shocked or disapproving; they are smug in accepting the violation of other women not in their circle.

There are many things that ought to be said about this issue. I do not have the space to address the issue of sexual abuse and the twisted rationalizations that allow for cover-up and protection of the perpetrator rather than protection for the victim. Let me clearly state it is utterly wrong and a grave sin before God that should be exposed and reported to the authorities. Victims are to be protected and lovingly cared for.

Another aspect of this, hard to name rightly but nonetheless a very present danger, is the competition, jealousy, and disregard of women leaders (and women in general) toward one another. Some of the most vicious attacks and accusations I have received as a woman in the pulpit have been from other women. I have been labeled unsubmitted, grandiose, a Jezebel, out of order, and rebellious because I have dared follow the call of God on my life. I have experienced both men and women standing up and walking out as I stepped behind the pulpit, thereafter only to receive letters and emails stating I am to be "silent in the church."

I am not bitter. I am mad at the enemy. The devil wants to keep us separated because when women come together, we change things. There is synergy in partnering together. Deuteronomy 32:30 explains this principle, asking, "How could one have chased a thousand, and two have put ten thousand to flight?" Deborah couldn't do what Jael did, and Jael couldn't do what Deborah did. Together they saved a nation. This is leadership in partnership—female and female.

What about men? Barak and Deborah fought side by side. Though a woman was credited with the defeat, Barak is remembered in Hebrews 11 as a man of faith. He honored the word of the Lord through Deborah and went out to meet the enemy even though they were severely out-weaponed. Likewise, when he asked Deborah to co-labor at his side, joining her gifts and authority with his, she said yes and rode out with the men. No berating. No reproach. No contempt. No belittling. No criticizing. No complaining. No comparing. No competing. This is leadership in partnership—female and male.

Think this through with me. When Jael killed Sisera, it wasn't because he was a man. Neither did she wait for her husband to get home to ask permission. No. When evil entered her sphere of leadership, she put a tent peg through its head. Not because she was rebellious, out of order, or unsubmitted, but because she had authority in her sphere and refused to allow the devil to enter there.

Deborah, Barak, Jael, and the army of Israel together defeated the enemy. Together they took dominion over evil in their land. Together we are better. This is leadership in partnership—male and female and God. From the beginning, male and female were given the call and commission of God together. Leadership is genderless.

In Genesis, God spoke to both Adam and Eve about the call on their lives.

> And God blessed them. And God said to them, "Be fruitful and multiply and fill the earth and subdue it, and have dominion over the fish of the sea and over the birds of the heavens and over every living thing that moves on the earth."[34]

God made humankind (male and female) in His image. As John Wesley explains, "Man[kind] was to be a creature different from all that had been hitherto made. Flesh and spirit, heaven and earth must be put together in him, and he must be allied to both worlds."[35] Being made in the image of God, allied to both heaven and earth, makes us the perfect creatures to have dominion over all He has created.

Dominion characterizes the call of leadership. As God's ally on the earth, the call to take dominion is to bear the responsibility to represent God and embody His work, will, and heart toward humanity and all of creation in word and deed. This is what you are called to. This is what we are all called to!

Wake up! Rise up! Dare to lead! Take back your voice, gifts, and call to lead in the places in which God has given you authority and influence. Take up your sword and your tent peg, for the Lord is about to sell the enemy *into the hands of women everywhere!*

5

Be Nobody's Fool!

THE STORY OF ABIGAIL

· 1 SAMUEL 25:1–39 ·

"Now therefore know this and consider what you should do."

1 Samuel 25:17

*T*HERE WAS NO TIME to sit back and ponder the situation. It was a crisis—a matter of life and death. Destruction was determined against her and her children by a man who had the power to make it happen. No one would be coming to her rescue, including her abusive husband, who had foolishly run off at the mouth and brought this upon them all. Fool that he was.

Where was he now? Partying and acting like the big man, the king of his own kingdom, with seemingly no cares in the world. His characteristic refusal to listen to reason from anyone, as everyone in the household knew, had instigated the current calamity. It was up to her—a woman—*his woman,* some might say—to "know and consider" what to do. Her decisions and actions would determine the future not only for her and hers, but also for the true king and his kingdom. She would be the deciding factor in this geopolitical power struggle.

Wait, what? Time out. Geopolitical power struggle? Isn't this the story of Abigail, the unsubmitted woman who, instead of following her husband's lead, went behind his back to get emotionally involved with another man? No, it isn't that story. And it isn't a romance novel either, though she ends up married to a real king.

The story of Abigail is strategically placed in the larger context of a season of epic change and transition in the nation of Israel. Power structures are in violent upheaval, and political intrigue abounds. Men are caught up in the thrills and horrors of war and mortal conflict, as happens when the seats of power are up for grabs. In fact, she is the only female among the five main characters in her story. She is the hero who moves the Kingdom of God forward. And lest we misunderstand, she is not the hero because of her gender (although God is making a point through her gender), but because of her character—her courage and her cunning—because of her *muchness.*

Signs and Times

"Nicki, go call Olly's doctor, *right now.* He is having trouble with his oxygenation." Nicki is my middle daughter. Only days before, she had given birth to the sweetest little baby boy, Oliver, who I now held in my arms. Olly had a shadowy blue ring around his lips and the faintest flaring of his nostrils upon each tiny breath.

Twenty-two years of working as an RN in pediatrics, NICU, and Labor and Delivery gave me an eye for trouble in infants. Now I held my own little grandson and saw the signs of distress. The ability to interpret symptoms, like reading signs, allowed me to make a proper assessment and act swiftly. I knew Olly needed help—*immediately.*

Nicki called the doctor and was told to bring Olly to the office as soon as physically possible—without passing "go," as we say in the board game Monopoly. The moment the doctor saw him, Oliver was admitted to the Neonatal Intensive Care Unit, where he would stay for ten days until he could sustain healthy oxygen levels without assistance. It was frightening. Nicki and I have often wondered what would have happened if I hadn't had the skill and training to read the signs of Olly's distress.

Signs convey information. They point, mark, remind, describe, welcome, and warn. They are messages that require not only our attention but also our interpretation to gain the insight contained in them. If we miss or misinterpret them, we fail to receive understanding needed to make decisions—sometimes critical decisions. Missing a sign can be fatal. Not only for us, but also for others.

Abigail's story begins with a sign contained in three seemingly innocuous words that could be easily overlooked, like the faint flaring of Oliver's nostrils: "Now Samuel died."[1] There they are. The three little words. Samuel's death was a sign of the times. God moves in times and seasons. The book of Ecclesiastes tells us there is an appointed time for everything under the sun. What's more, for every divinely appointed time, there is a divinely appointed, corresponding, and appropriate action.

Why? God created time to accommodate His every purpose and plan.[2]

Think about this for a moment. Every minute, day, month, year, and lifetime are given by God to accommodate and accomplish His purpose and plan in (and through) our lives. The psalmist says it this way: "Your eyes saw my unformed body; all the days ordained for me were written in your book before one of them came to be."[3] Each moment is pregnant with divine purpose for us. Each moment is divinely appointed. God has arranged it.

Samuel's death signals a *now* time. "Behold, I am doing a new thing; *now* it springs forth, do you not perceive it?" says the prophet Isaiah.[4] A now time is when God intervenes in history in a dramatic way, introducing something new. It is a time of major transition (that dreaded word).

Samuel is the last of the prophets who governed Israel. So, his death is monumental. It means God is introducing a new kind of government with a new kind of leader. This is not the first time this has happened. Before the prophets were the judges, and before the judges were the patriarchs who ruled. The death of Samuel signals closure—of his life and trusted leadership for sure, but more important, of an entire era. It screams, "There will be no going back! There is *now* both a spiritual and political shift." An entire nation is thrust into transition, forced to navigate epic change without Samuel's guidance.

In times of transition, when new things (leaders, organizations, relationships, paradigms) are being birthed, established, and positioned, there are old things being removed, left behind, put aside, or re-created. Lines are drawn. The old, as it is, cannot be brought into the new. Loyalties and allegiances are tested. It is a tumultuous and even dangerous time.

Tale of Two Kings

Before we talk about Abigail and what her story means for women, we must first talk about the men. Men are always part of our stories, just as we are always part of theirs. For God made humankind in His image, male and female He created them, to partner and care for what He created and to reveal His nature and love to others.[5]

There are four men important to our story. Samuel is one. The transition from prophets to kings was in process but not fully completed when Samuel died. "Then David rose," says the text. David, the shepherd boy and prophesied king, will play a major part in this story. Another principal character lay behind the scenes, never mentioned by name. Saul. *King* Saul, to be exact.

Good-looking Saul, head and shoulders above all others, who fell short in kingly resolve. He obeyed half-heartedly, and God was sorry He had made Saul king. God rejected him, instructing Samuel to anoint David as king in his place. Never mind the fact that Saul was still on the throne! By the time we are introduced to Abigail, David has been forced into exile in the face of Saul's murderous rage. David and Saul are like two clashing kingdoms or political parties: one outgoing and one incoming. God is moving, bringing a new thing. The new thing is a new king—David, a boy who is unlike Saul in almost every conceivable way. Perhaps Samuel could have resolved the conflict, but he's dead, and we are left watching how this will play out. We are left, as well, with a contrast and comparison of two kings.

Saul had position and title but no anointing. To be king in this era, one must be appointed by God and anointed by the Holy Spirit through the prophet of God. The Spirit of God had been removed from Saul due to his disobedience to God's command.

111

The authority he clings to is positional only. The Bible captures the drama:

> "You have rejected the word of the LORD, and the LORD has rejected you from being king over Israel." As Samuel turned to go away, Saul seized the skirt of his robe, and it tore. And Samuel said to him, "The LORD has torn the kingdom of Israel from you this day and has given it to a neighbor of yours, who is better than you."[6]

"You have done a foolish thing," Samuel scolds. Saul's fear of failure led to his disobedience that led him into the failure he feared. Selah.

David had the anointing of the Spirit and the prophetic word of the Lord regarding his role as king, but no position or title. He already held a measure of notoriety among the people for his valiance in battle. Songs celebrating his valor and skill as a warrior were being sung, "Saul has struck down his thousands, and David his ten thousands."[7] These songs incited the deadly jealousy of Saul, forcing David to flee for his life. He could have assassinated Saul more than a few times, but David didn't allow ambition to overtake him. He refused to lift his hand against Saul to greedily grasp what was prophesied, though he had many opportunities. It would be by the hand of God, or it would not be.

As with every move of God, a line is drawn in the sand that tests the heart of men—and women. Enter Nabal and Abigail.

Nabal and Abigail

"Now the name of the man was Nabal, and the name of his wife Abigail. The woman was discerning and beautiful, but the man was harsh and badly behaved; he was a Calebite."[8] Observe that the man and the woman are introduced by name in the same sentence. They are being contrasted and compared. Note, they are not being pitted against each other. It is true that the woman in this story is the one who chooses the better path, but it isn't at the expense of the men in the story. It is important you understand that. Each character in the story has freedom and autonomy to make choices. Each is given opportunity to do what is right and good and is held personally responsible for the choices they make and the communal effects of those choices.

The contrast and comparison is striking in these two short sentences. The author is very intentional to emphasize that the *name* of the man is Nabal, and the *name* of his wife is Abigail. Names in Scripture are signs. If we discover the interpretation, we find its message. In the Hebrew culture, naming involves proclaiming, even prophesying, the nature, heritage, and prophetic promise of a person. Sometimes names describe the circumstances surrounding his or her birth. She is beautiful, comely; he is surly, mean. She has a good mind, deep intelligence; he is thoughtless, a fool.

In our story, Nabal's name means "fool." Abigail's name means "the father's joy."[9] It is the intention of the author for us to understand that from this point forward, what is revealed about these two people in relationship to character and behavior is either foolish or pleasing to God. Nabal and Abigail will portray for us foolishness and wisdom.

In staccato fashion, Scripture gives us several details about the man. All of them tell his story. He was rich [*me'od*], meaning he was extremely wealthy. While Abigail had muchness, Nabal, the foolish one, had nothing but these many riches. He had land, servants, and thousands of sheep and goats. He was a Calebite,[10] meaning he was a descendant of Caleb who was renown as one of the twelve spies sent out by Moses to spy out the Promised Land. Of the twelve, Caleb was one of two who came back with an encouraging word for the people. He followed the Lord for the whole of his life, surviving the forty years in the wilderness and inheriting a portion of the Promised Land while full of vigor in his eighties.[11]

With all his wealth and lineage, Nabal would be counted a chieftain in his tribe, giving him political power, influence, and prestige. Yet, he was named Nabal. Fool. What loving mother or father would give their innocent infant son a name that means fool, labeling his future with a curse? None. Not one. No, Nabal had made a name for himself, and Scripture declares it. He was not like his father, Caleb, nor his forefather Abraham. For all his wealth, lineage, power, and prestige, he was a foolish man. It is only the foolish man who makes a name for himself rather than allowing God to make his name great.[12] And in that way, he betrays his own family's legacy, spoiling his inheritance as a son of Caleb.

What is a fool? A fool is someone who does not recognize God's right to rule (authority), who does not know, or perhaps, does not *want* to know, God. He is someone who lives by his own standards.[13]

A fool is characterized prolifically in Scripture as angry, proud, arrogant, disobedient, self-centered, greedy, emotionally driven, unwise, and spiritually blind. There is more, but the picture is clear. Nabal is a fool, and his foolishness is not only revealed by his name but also by his rash, selfish, abusive, and cruel behavior.

There is another sign found in the naming sequence. As soon as the man's name is given, his wife begins to take precedence for her wisdom. His name is given first, but his character is named second. Her name is given second, but her character is named first. Nabal's foolishness is exposed in the telling of it in subjugated position. Wisdom is always exalted. Foolishness is always humbled.

Abigail is described in three short details in the introduction. She is discerning, beautiful, and married to an abusive fool. Notice, being married to a fool has not made her one. We know nothing of how the story will unfold, but we are now set up to expect something from her that we will not get from him. A person, male or female, may be wise or foolish, yet it matters in this story that it is the woman embodying wisdom. In many of the biblical stories, God reveals the feminine gender as capable, wise, understanding, bold, and tenacious. These stories redeem this gender from the plague of cultural and theological misinterpretations that result in the mislabeling of women.

Now it seems we know all we need to know about our fourth man and Abigail. Something is about to happen. Something important. Nabal and Abigail, in the course of their daily lives, are about to come face-to-face with the *new* move of God and the new man of God.

The Fool and His Foolishness

Feasting is always an anticipated event at shearing time. Sheep and goats are bleating. Servants are sweating, shearing, and caring for them all. For wealthy chieftains, it is an abundant affair with plentiful provisions to spare. Everyone knows this—including robbers. Even the wealthy can use a little protection, unsolicited as it may be. In return, they can give a little from all that abundance. After all, doesn't one considerable favor deserve another? As one chieftain to another, it certainly would be the polite thing to do.

Well, you know what they say about assumptions. Ten young men stand before Nabal, in David's name, explaining the favor of protection done for him. They come with a direct message from their leader: "Therefore let my young men find favor in your eyes, for we come on a feast day. Please give whatever you have at hand to your servants and to your son David."[14] Dramatic pause.

This is it. The moment of testing I told you about. The line is drawn in the sand by this request. Choices will now need to be made revealing loyalties and allegiances, whether each perceives what God is doing, and whether they are willing to adjust their lives accordingly.

Nabal mocks the request and requestor, disdainfully retorting, "Who is David? Who is the son of Jesse? There are many servants these days who are breaking away from their masters. Shall I take my bread . . . and give it to men who come from I do not know where?"[15] His reply exposes his vanity and the shallowness of his thinking. He is too foolish to recognize that the glory of God rests on the humble, so he is insulted by David's modesty and smallness.

He is consumed with his pride. *How dare this fellow approach me like an equal! Who does he think he is? He could have made a name for himself had he stayed with Saul, the king. He isn't worth my time, much less my wealth. He is a beggar, a runaway slave, an insolent dog, and he can remain one. He brings nothing of value to my table, and I will bring nothing of all that I have to his.*

Nabal is unaware of the testing of his heart. He does not discern the moment. Like the foolish man in Jesus' parable, he fails to recognize that his soul is about to be required of him. He is rude, inhospitable, unyielding, and superior. He makes a fool of himself. This is what fools do. And as Scripture warns, because he is a fool, his prosperity destroys him.[16]

His response is not only proud, but remarkably selfish. "Why should I take *my* bread and water and the meat *I* have slaughtered for *my* shearers?" His response is incredibly insulting. "And give it to men who come from who knows where?" But what is most troubling, what is truly satanic, is the accusation it holds: "Who is David? He is no more than a runaway slave."

The accusation is rooted in selfish ambition. It has cultural and political purpose. For Nabal to acknowledge David's request would mean to have recognized David at least as an equal or, more akin to the truth, as a superior worthy of support. This would obligate Nabal to David. It would mean establishing an allegiance—a loyalty. Aligning with David would mean disloyalty to Saul.

Nabal rejects the offer with spite, making a show of his disgust at David and his story. He will not acknowledge or submit to this upstart leader. Nabal has taken up Saul's side and offense. He surely thought that remaining loyal to Saul would garner him favor with the rejected king; however, it only aligns him with the prophecy and its fulfillment spoken by the prophet to Saul. Saul, as Samuel said, "had done foolishly," and the kingdom was already torn from him. Rejecting David, therefore, is Nabal's last and perhaps most foolish choice.

He returns to his opulent party. Like Saul and unlike David, Nabal did not wrestle or seek the Lord for revelation concerning his decision. His pride and self-indulgence dulled his ability to discern the time. He was completely unaware that everything he possessed and the people under his protection were in grave danger.

Scripture warns us to be careful when we "have eaten and are full" or when we live in ease and prosperity.[17] Those are the most dangerous times. We are tempted to think we gained it all by our own efforts and forget God. As individuals, as a people, or as a nation, we become blind to what God has done and is doing on our behalf. We lose spiritual discernment. We become dull to the Spirit's leading, or worse, we become apostate. We become more protective of our positions and possessions and less protective of our heart for God. We may end up getting all we ever dreamed of, but not all God ever dreamed for us. And that means our lives will be a nightmare for others, especially the most vulnerable and the most desperate.

The Bride and Her Muchness

The foolish insult was of the kind that cannot go unanswered by a chieftain of equal or superior rank. A runaway slave? Men with questionable pedigree in a culture in which bloodlines equal honor? The servants overhearing the message sent to David understood what this would provoke and the kind of sword David wielded—even if the fool did not. There is no reasoning with a fool. He won't listen. Rescue would have to come from another place. Tell Abigail—she hears.

> But one of the young men [servants] told Abigail, Nabal's wife, "Behold, David sent messengers out of the wilderness to greet our master, and he railed at them. . . . *Now therefore know this and consider what you should do*, for harm is determined against our master and against all his house, and he is such a worthless man that one cannot speak to him."[18]

Harm is determined. It is a crisis of life and death. Killing the fool would not be the end of it. The sword would slice through the entire household, leaving no living male of any age—fathers, brothers, sons, or servants. Decisions must be made *now*. Time

118

is suffocatingly short. What to do will require *knowing and considering*, which is to do what fools do not do. But Abigail is no fool. And she is vindicated by her wisdom.

We know the folly of fools. They think they are in control. They are not looking to perceive the right action for the divinely appointed time. Fools hate knowledge and refuse to listen.[19] And the more foolish they are, the surer they are that they are not foolish. They have been deceived into thinking they already have the knowledge they need, and others should listen to them. They presume that *their* grasp of God's will is the only grasp that matters.

Women in Abigail's day seldom had much control or choice. She had no recourse to change her situation. What's more, though he was an abusive fool, Nabal was a key to the survival and preservation of her family. His status afforded protection, and his wealth a measure of autonomy. She would not harm him. She was a wise and discerning woman who spent her life in the service of her family, and even her husband.

The wisdom of the wise is to be concerned with every life, foolish or not, in the godly hope that the eyes of the fool may be enlightened and his path be narrowed away from destruction. The wise know that God is sovereign and brings rain on the just and the unjust. They selflessly give, love, and serve others. And they look to God for answers and perspective.

Now the sword is approaching quickly. She knows the cutting down of every male emasculates a household, undermining its ability to defend itself in battle, provide for the household, and produce progeny. It is no accident in Abigail's story that the woman will step up to protect the lives of men. Women in Scripture often do.

In the book of Exodus, Pharaoh ordered the midwives to kill every male Hebrew child at birth. He knew a nation without men was easier to control and enslave. The female midwives, with courage and cunning, risked their lives to defy the order and save the boys. Still more ironic, Pharaoh's own daughter saved three-month-old Moses as he floated by her in the river—the one who would deliver the very people her father killed and enslaved. Now it is Abigail's turn to join the ranks of the women who stepped out of their culturally dictated boundaries and find her *muchness*.

The revealing of Abigail's wisdom begins with the servant's report. He knew she would listen. Abigail's wisdom includes a willingness to hear those who come to her with a message, even a servant, because wisdom is never dictated by gender, social status, ethnicity, or education. Sometimes it comes in the most unexpected package.

When David's home at Ziklag is burned to the ground and his wives and children are captured by enemies, God told him to pursue without more detail.[20] He needs intel and direction. On pursuit, he comes upon a near-dead Egyptian slave left to die on the road. David, like the good Samaritan in Luke 10:30–33, cares for him. Unbeknownst to David, this man had the very information he needed. Sometimes the wisdom we need comes in very unexpected packages. It is wisdom to treat others with respect and listen to what they have to say. Nabal does not have ears to hear; Abigail does.

The servant exhorts Abigail to *de'ah*[21] and *raah*[22] (Hebrew for "know" and "consider") what she will do. Knowing refers to the mental process of knowing or learning through facts and information. The word *consider* in our passage means "to see and perceive with a divine or revelatory perspective." Prophets are sometimes called "*raah*," or "seers," in Scripture—those who see as God *sees*. The God whom Hagar named as the God who sees.[23] Those who *raah* see with prophetic insight or foresight according to God's perspective. In other words, Abigail will need revelatory wisdom and shrewdness to rescue her household.

Jesus tells a story of a man threatened with economic crisis who allows adversity to stimulate creative strategies to help him thrive in trouble.[24] He sees what is coming and uses his resources and position to take advantage of the situation. Jesus ends the parable saying, "For the sons of this world are more shrewd in dealing with their own generation than the sons of light."[25]

Jesus exhorts His sons and daughters to be shrewd. To *be shrewd* means to "have the wisdom and prophetic perception to assess every situation and circumstance to act with wisdom, sound judgement and foresight which will direct or re-direct the outcome."[26] Thanks to the wisdom and creativity of God, there is always an opportunity hidden in the crisis. The Spirit gives us the gift of shrewdness so that we can see that opportunity and know how to make the most of it.

Did you see the movie some years back called *Hidden Figures*?[27] In the 1960s, America was in the throes of great change, racial division, turmoil, and transition. Katherine G. Johnson, Dorothy Vaughan, and Mary Jackson—all marginalized women of color—managed to see beyond the resistance and the limits placed on them and stepped into the opportunity no one else saw. They were shrewd, bold, clever, and courageous. They had *muchness*.

Abigail knows the current trouble brought by her husband's folly. There will be destruction if she cannot *see* the opportunity within the crisis. We shall soon see what she sees. The story advances swiftly to convey urgency. Food for an army is gathered and sent by donkey to David within two verses. In the third, she is meeting David, who is dressed for battle and hungry for blood.

Read too fast and you will miss the little sentence tucked within those three verses: "But she did not tell her husband Nabal."[28] By making a decision and acting on it, in opposition to what the male head of the house had decided, Abigail breaks with the sociocultural conventions and limitations for females of her day. Yet, one of the things she *knows* is that asking permission of a fool is foolish. Though it may come at an awful price at the hands of an enraged David or a cruel Nabal, she chooses to act on behalf of others, not securing her own welfare alone.

Now we will witness her shrewdness, her wisdom—her muchness. We will see what she saw. She throws herself facedown before him and lifts up her voice. This wealthy woman, with land and servants enough to feed an army, humbles herself as a vassal before a lord; or more to the point, before a *king*. She transfers the guilt of her husband onto herself, asks forgiveness, and then reveals what she has perceived.

> "For the LORD will certainly make my lord a sure house, because my lord is fighting the battles of the LORD. . . . *And when the LORD has done to my lord according to all the good that he has spoken concerning you and has appointed you prince over Israel,* my lord shall have no cause of grief or pangs of conscience for having shed blood without cause or for my lord working salvation himself."[29]

We do not know how she knows it, but Abigail, no less than Nabal, knows David's circumstances and what has been prophesied about him. Unlike her husband, she has discerned the signs and perceives that David is God's new chosen one, the new sovereign appointed and anointed by God. She approaches not only beseeching forgiveness for the insults of her husband, but her actions tell of something more—humility and submission to a divinely appointed king, the rightful ruler and savior. Her king. She recognizes what God is doing and says "Amen" to it.

Abigail is affirming David as the anointed of the Lord. In her wisdom and shrewdness, she breaks with the fool and his folly, who maintains his loyalty and allegiance to Saul. This was not a refusal to submit to her husband; it was submission to God first and foremost. Whatever the cost. She wasn't acting without hope but was willing to risk the consequences at hand and at home, leaving the outcome in God's hands. She knew, as David himself did, that it is better to fall into the hands of God than to fall into the hands of men. This is the fear of the Lord, the beginning of wisdom.

Loyalty and allegiance to God comes before all others. At times, the cost we pay will be some type of martyrdom in relationship or reputation. In the least, it risks misunderstanding. At most, it risks the loss of our lives. God knows the outcome. He knew the cost of Abigail's actions.

The Cost of Foolishness and the Reward of Wisdom

What happens to Nabal isn't pretty and certainly isn't desirable. It is a sign and a warning. Foolishness begins with self as the source and culminates in disloyalty to God expressed by disobedience. It always ends, as it does for Saul, with the kingdom torn from you.

Nabal has done foolishly. Yet, every male in his household will not be cut down, as David warned. Only one, Nabal. In spite of all his power, position, and possessions, the fool in his folly will not be a chieftain participating in the new move of God, in the kingdom under King David. He is dead. It is the end of his story. The kingdom is torn from him.

The description of his demise is interesting:

In the morning, when the wine had gone out of Nabal, his wife told him these things, and his heart died within him, and he became as a stone. And about ten days later the LORD struck Nabal, and he died. . . . Then David sent and spoke to Abigail, to take her as his wife.[30]

The wine goes, the heart goes, the life goes, and finally the bride goes. In Scripture, wine is the prophetic symbol for the covenant blessings of God, who promises to provide for and sustain His people. In the New Testament it is also a sign of joy and celebration for God's people.[31] God blesses and sustains the faithful.

The heart is the place where God looks to find where our loyalties and allegiance (faithfulness) lie. God rejected both Saul and David's brothers as king in favor of David, saying, "For the LORD sees not as man sees: man looks on the outward appearance, but the LORD looks on the heart."[32] Folly hardens the heart. Pharaoh hardened his heart when God, through Moses, told him to let His people go. His hardening of heart cost him every firstborn among his people, including his own son. Death comes to a hard heart.

God is always working to heal and redeem hardened hearts. He does not condemn or randomly and capriciously reject. What He rejects is what we are making of ourselves when we consistently and persistently reject His will for our lives, choosing to live life our own way, in stubborn sin and unrepentant disobedience. As we persist in our resistance to God's will, remaining indifferent to those in need, we lock ourselves more and more deeply into foolishness, hardening our hearts and darkening our minds. Finally, then, God comes against us in force, making one last attempt at arresting our attention.

Life does not belong to man, but to God, who alone can give it. In the beginning, He gave humanity life, then His own life by the Spirit through the Son. Jesus sealed the life God gives us for eternity when He shed His blood on the cross and was raised to life again. All things have their life in the trinitarian God—Father, Son, and Spirit. Without Him, the life that has an impact on the world for eternity is dead, for it has no lasting life of its own.

The Bride, the people of God, are those who proliferate the life of Christ, bearing sons and daughters, ever expanding God's Kingdom. She is eternally being set free from every enslavement and cruel bondage.

The fool is dead. All property, people, and possession are now in the hands of Abigail, considerably increasing her external value. She owns a significant portion of land in Hebron, giving her influence among chieftains. David is wise to marry her and expand his political and national influence. David sees God's providence and favor on this woman and how it helps position him. David is no fool. Neither is Abigail. She, with all her muchness, is the Father's pleasure.

Muchness, Not Seductress

Abigail is so brave, so brilliantly savvy in this dangerous story. She stood on a razor's edge. If she had been one minute too late, if she'd hesitated for one moment, or if she'd given in to insecurity and inadequacy saying to herself, *I'm only a girl. What can I do?* they would all have been dead. Abigail saved her people through her courage and ability to *know* and *consider*. She didn't try to seduce David as Jezebel tried to seduce Jehu. She was shrewd, subtle, but not treacherous or unchaste.

And besides the wisdom she displayed, there is something more in her story worth savoring. As Abigail humbled herself at the feet of her king, asking his pardon for her husband's folly and asserting the efficacy of the prophecy that he will indeed be king, she interjects an incredibly insightful word of counsel: "My lord shall have no cause of grief or pangs of conscience for having shed blood without cause or for my lord working salvation himself."[33] You can feel David's breath suck in.

He, himself, suddenly sees what Abigail sees. He'd had opportunities to take the throne by his own hand, taking his own revenge rather than leaving it in God's hands, yet had refused them. He knew that vengeance belonged to God. Had he done to Nabal what he'd intended, he would have been guilty of murder. Abigail not only saved her household, but in a sense also saves David, preserving his innocence and purity before the Lord. In her wisdom, she helped preserve the move of God and its purity. She not only saves David from a fool, as his friend Jonathan had so often delivered him from Saul, but more important, she saves him from his own foolishness.

God celebrates the courage, cunning, and leadership of women, correcting long-held misconceptions in the Church that have inspired mistreatment, unsolicited suspicion, and unjustified barricades for women. Scripture is canceling the notion that strong and resourceful women are the cause of problems in the Garden and in the Church, forever to be held at arm's length, closely monitored for anticipated seductions of men. No. God raises women with muchness and sends them to do His will, working salvation for households, communities, nations, and even kings.

I prophesy that women, once unjustly theologically accused of bringing impurity to the Church and restrained from operating in the call and gifts God has ordained for them, will be loosed in our lifetime in great numbers. Anointed and wise women who have allowed the fiery opposition and the challenges of the past and present to purify their hearts, cultivate humility, and foster dependence upon God will be called upon, in large number, to partner in the moves of God in their generations. And the foolish men around them will not be able to hinder them or stop what God has started.

6

Let Go

JOCHEBED'S STORY

· EXODUS 1:22–2:6 ·

Women become the saviors of early Israel and bring on the
redemption from Egypt.[1]

*G*IRL, YOU CAN DO HARD THINGS." I imagine this
is what Jochebed, the consummate mother, would say to
us after taking our face into her hands and looking straight into
our eyes. She would be preparing us to hear her story. Maybe
she said the same to her three children, who grew up to become
notable and noble prophetic leaders of Israel. If she didn't say it,
she certainly lived it. I imagine it was from her that they learned
to do hard things.

Hearing and embracing the message of this unflinchingly courageous woman may be doing a hard thing for some. And yet, Jochebed's story will settle for us that doing hard things, though not easy nor cheap, means doing right things that often have unexpected and sometimes profound outcomes in the providence of God. Her story is crucial in our quest to find our muchness— our "very-much" strength, total capacity, and the fullness of our God-given power that sometimes gets lost in life's confusions, troubles, and uncertainties. As we listen to the message of Jochebed's story, we will be invited to do hard things. And we can, because muchness is a part of who we already are, what is in each of us. It is how we love God and accomplish everything for which we are created. Yes. *We can do hard things.*

The Promise of Exodus

Our story begins in the opening chapters of the book of Exodus, the second book of the Pentateuch, which are the five books historically understood to be written by Moses to the people of Israel during their wilderness wanderings. The book begins by naming the descendants of Jacob, who were sustained through a great famine by moving to Egypt, where Joseph, one of Jacob's twelve sons, had become second only to the Pharaoh then in charge. In the era in which our story takes place, Joseph is no longer alive. Neither is Jacob, any of his other sons, or any of that generation. What was alive, however, was the promise of God.

The Lord had said to Jacob (called Israel because he wrestled with God and won) many years before, "Fear not to go down into Egypt; for I will there make of thee a great nation."[2] Abraham, the great patriarch who by faith left everything he had ever known— his country, his family, his life—to follow God, was told by the

Lord that his descendants, of whom Jacob was one, would be like the sand of the sea or the stars of the sky and be a great multitude of nations.[3] Going back even further, we discover that in the Garden, God also blessed Adam and Eve to be fruitful and multiply.[4] This was a thread of promise found woven throughout Genesis.

So, when the book of Exodus opens by saying, "The children of Israel were fruitful, and increased abundantly, and multiplied, and waxed exceeding mighty; and the land was filled with them,"[5] the author is pulling on that thread. The promise of God was very much alive and active, as God's prophetic promises are. (An interesting note about that opening line about Israel's fruitfulness is the use of the word for *muchness*. In Hebrew, "waxed exceedingly mighty" is written as "*me'od, me'od.*" In their multitudinous numbers, they had *muchness*—exceeding might.) The truth for us to hear is that what God said, He is still saying. His word never dies. It is eternally alive and acting to effect God's wonderous intentions for godly good.[6]

As exciting as it is to see the promises of God being fulfilled, there was something more, which was also something hard. When God prophetically promised Abraham that his seed (descendants) would become a multitude of nations, He also prophesied they would become strangers in a foreign land, enslaved and afflicted for four hundred years.[7] This prophecy was also alive and active. It came to pass after Joseph died because the new pharaoh was not Joseph's friend. He feared the muchness of Joseph's people, the people of Israel. So, in his fear, he enslaved them. Day after day they were subjected to cruel labor under pitiless taskmasters.

When we approach Jochebed's story, the lives of her people have been narrowed by bitter injustice and merciless oppression. Yet, even as the agony of their suffering pierces our hearts, we are also buoyed by hope. The prophecy about something hard—

slavery and affliction—was not the end of what God had prophesied. Something good, profoundly good, would come after. He said, "I will bring judgment on the nation that they serve, and afterward they shall come out with great possessions."[8] It is a promise He means to keep. It is a thread of promise that will not be broken. Hope and trust in God and His word helps His people do hard things—without their hearts becoming hard.

Irony

Scripture loves irony. The Holy Spirit, as the One inspiring the writing, must have a wicked sense of humor. Not "wicked," as in "evil," mind you. Rather, "wicked" in the way American northeasterners use the word, meaning something more like intensely and extremely "smaht" ("smart" for you West Coast people) or witty. Irony in a story is often created when we, the readers, are aware of an outcome of which the characters are unaware. *Merriam-Webster* defines it as "a situation that is strange or funny because things happen in a way that seems to be the opposite of what is expected."[9]

If you were not aware, Exodus is a story about Moses and the most significant deliverance event in all of the Old Testament. In the big picture, it is the story of the fulfillment of the prophetic promises mentioned above. Moses is the deliverer God will raise up to deliver His people from their enslavement in Egypt. Moses, however, is yet to be born at this point in our story.

In the first fourteen verses, the book opens by telling us the names of influential men, namely the sons of Jacob, and puts us in remembrance of the prophetic promises given to the patriarchs Abraham and Jacob. We have also learned that another man, unnamed and known only by his position and title, has enslaved and oppressed God's people due to his fear of their strength and numbers. We are allowed to think, for a moment, that the only suitable deliverers of God's people, the only suitable recipients of God's prophetic promises, and the only suitable agents of defiance to oppressors and systems of oppression are men.

"God always has the right man in the right place at the right time,"[10] one commentator of Exodus announced. This gave me a chuckle. It wasn't that it was an incorrect conclusion as it pertains to Moses, but that it was somewhat ironic considering the story I was about to tell and the characters that would be included. It is also ironic because in the first chapters of our story, and indeed, at many critical points throughout salvation history, God *also* always has the right *woman* in the right place at the right time. God intentionally highlights this for us as the seminal events of the great Exodus story unfold. God desires our understanding of His providence to be Spirit-formed and informed regarding where we find ourselves positioned in everyday life, whether domestic, business, ministry, or any other. We are always, at all times, on a divinely appointed mission.

All the men have been named, signaling that God has made good on His prophetic words. The unnamed pharaoh fears that God's people will either turn against or leave him. He cannot countenance either, so he attempts to stunt their growth by interrupting both occasion and drive to "be fruitful and multiply." Good plan, except that it does not work. Ironically, the more they are oppressed, the more they multiply. Pharaoh's plan cannot overturn God's providence, prophecies, and promise. His word is no match for God's.

Because his heart is hardened by arrogance and long disobedience, Pharaoh is not ready to relent. He has no fear of God, only of God's people. His fear does not allow him to loosen his grip and let go. Instead, he makes a fist and devises a second, more odious plan. He decrees murder by the hand of those called and skilled in deliverance. He calls in the midwives who serve the Hebrew women in giving birth. He offloads his diabolical death sentence onto the very ones dedicated to bringing forth life—women on both sides of the birthing stool. As they attend the mother giving birth, they are to kill any sons that are born. If the woman gives birth to a daughter, they are to let her live.

Killing the boys will emasculate the Israelites. Boys fight. Boys are the strength of the nation. Boys pass on the family line. Boys grow up to be warriors, leaders, and deliverers. Killing the boys will stunt the growth and blunt the strength of those he fears yet needs to build his kingdom. Girls don't fight. Girls are powerless. Girls are insignificant. Girls are not a threat. Let them live.

Pharaoh didn't seem to know much about girls. What he assumes about them here, well, you know what they say about assumptions. He assumes all the above about women *and* that the midwives will bow down in fearful obedience to his edicts. But Scripture tells us they feared the One greater than Pharaoh. The fear of the Lord catalyzed their shrewd defiance of the tyrant's murderous plot, despite the real risk, in concert with their commitment to life and family preservation. When confronted, they devised an explanation playing on Pharaoh's arrogant superiority and racial bias, saying, "Hebrew women are not like Egyptian women." They exploited his racism by contrasting the slaves to native-born Egyptians. Indeed, in the original Hebrew, the midwives call the Hebrew women "animals,"[11] insinuating their robustness in the birthing process was because they were almost less than human and certainly a far cry from the delicate femininity of Egyptian women.

Again, ironically, thanks to God's wry sense of humor, Pharaoh's attempted infant pogrom results in *more* births, increased *me'od*, and the building up of the household of these so-called non-threatening women, the midwives, who demonstrated *muchness*—courage and cunning in their defiance of Pharaoh. Disobedience is not always rebellion. Sometimes it is righteousness and faith.[12] God rewards righteousness and faithfulness.

Before moving on from the shrewd midwives, it is significant that their story highlights the conflict in Exodus between the powerful and the powerless. Take notice that the midwives stand in the royal chambers and defy the pharaoh just as Moses and Aaron eventually will do. The midwives, the women, set the precedent.[13] Pharaoh, the ruler of Egypt, is defied by a group of powerless, insignificant girls. Go figure.

This was now the second time Pharaoh had tried to stop God's word from coming to pass. As an Egyptian Pharaoh, he was raised to think he was a god; therefore, his word was the word of a god. He was not a god, he was no match for God, and neither was his word, but he won't find that out definitively for several more chapters. He doesn't yet know he is not fighting the people of Israel; he is fighting their God. He doesn't yet know that he must let God's people go.

Pharaoh decides he cannot let it go; his fear and arrogance won't allow it. It blinds him to the irony of what is happening. He doubles down. As if it was not enough for him to hire midwives for infanticide, he employs his whole kingdom for murder. He makes a jaw-dropping, heart-stopping, breath-robbing command: "Every son that is born to the Hebrews you shall cast into the Nile, but you shall let every daughter live."[14] Evil is never satisfied. As Israel grows in giving birth to life, so does Egypt in giving birth to death.

The Woman

> Now a man from the house of Levi went and took as his wife a Levite woman. The woman conceived and bore a son, and when she saw that he was a fine child, she hid him three months.[15]

Talk about irony. On the heels of a death decree for Hebrew boys born in Egypt, we stumble headlong over two sentences, spoken as if it is a fine day in the kingdom, until the full stop at the last five words, when it is apparent something is amiss. If it weren't for the hiding, we may have thought we'd escaped the harrowing murder plot. We haven't, but the author of this passage doesn't seem to be worried. Instead, we get the sense that all is well and under control (and not by Pharaoh). We are being assured of that truth every step of the way.

As we are introduced to the future deliverer (more irony here), he needs deliverance. His birth has placed him and his mother in a vulnerable position because they are powerless to change their circumstances. This is something familiar to the human experience. Living within familial, societal, or governmental systems in which we find ourselves vulnerable and powerless in temporary or prolonged circumstances set in motion by powerbrokers is familiar to us all. The temptation is to give in to fear and turn back, turn away, give up, or give in to living as dead.

In just such a dire circumstance, we meet *the woman*. She has a name that can be found in other books, but she remains unnamed in her most heroic moments. It has been said in other chapters of this book but it bears repeating: The unnamed woman is every woman and all women. Scripture leaves room for each of us to be found in the story of unnamed women. They were risk takers—courageous, assertive, and shrewd. Scripture wants us to believe they are us, and we are them.

Several significant unnamed women, by their muchness, stood up to power, influenced the political elite, effected deliverance for their families, cities, and nation, and preserved covenant history. The unnamed wise woman of Abel ended the bloody pursuit of a fugitive by influencing leaders, through skilled conflict negotiations, to send his head over the wall into the hands of his pursuer.[16] The unnamed widow at Zarephath fed her last meal to the prophet she did not know, trusting the word of the Lord in his mouth, thus receiving miraculous provision by faith.[17] The unnamed woman with the issue of blood (code for "unclean") fought through a crowd to touch the hem of Jesus' garment, believing He was the Messiah who was able to heal her, and Jesus commended her for her faith.[18] The unnamed Samaritan (code for "outcast") woman at the well did not flinch at the exposure of her reality by Jesus, and so received one of the most essential understandings of the Kingdom. She then evangelized her entire town.[19]

The unnamed woman in our story finds herself embroiled in trouble and treachery. We are to identify with her as those who, at some time in our journey, will face similar circumstances as we follow Jesus. She is us. We are her. And at times, we are also vulnerable, powerless, and tempted to turn away, turn back, or turn inward with fear. Others may not know our name, and we ourselves may momentarily forget it, but God does not. He has been given the name that is above every other name because He is always only faithful and never forgets us.

The woman in our story is Jochebed. She is a slave woman born in a priestly line that would ordinarily have given her honor and favor, yet she is powerless to change her circumstances in her degraded state. For three months, she has managed to hide Moses from the hands of those who would callously toss him into the great Nile River, worshiped by the Egyptians as a source of life, to be swallowed up by death. Tension, like her son's infant body from conception, had grown beyond the point of hiddenness, unbearably proclaiming that his life hung in the balance, teetering on the point of no return, to be tipped in either direction depending on *her*. The woman. The mother. Not her husband. Not her father. Not her brother. Her. (Now, as readers, we know someone else, someone *Other*, is also at work supernaturally overseeing the events.) Still, her choices at this very moment will influence the story's direction for her, her children, and her people.

Build the Boat

If the rabbinic scholars are correct, Jochebed is no stranger to danger, nor is she a coward. The rabbis identify Jochebed with Shiphrah, one of the two Hebrew midwives mentioned earlier in our story.[20] Remember, God rewarded Shiphrah for her actions by establishing her household (*battim* in the original Hebrew) and giving her her own children.[21] Moses, her own son, is the reward for her faithful and righteous defiance of Pharaoh. Assuming she is Shiphrah, the midwife, she refused to kill the children of others, and she will not now turn in fear of Pharaoh to stand in agreement with this ungodly command to murder the fruit of her fear of the Lord. She will not sacrifice her heavenly reward on the altar of self-preservation. God, not Pharaoh, gave this child. And Pharaoh is not the only one with a plan. She reaches to take hold of what was in her hand—reeds and tar.

What can one do with such things? Build a boat, described in our passage as an "ark." The word used for the floating basket Jochebed weaves is used one other time in the Old Testament. Can you guess where? In the story of the great Flood that washed away all hope of surviving for any but those tucked into the ark built by Noah according to divine blueprint. "By faith Noah, being warned by God concerning events as yet unseen, in reverent fear constructed an ark for the saving of his household."[22]

The fear of the Lord in the life of Noah resulted in saving his household. The fear of the Lord in the life of Jochebed built hers. Perhaps she remembered Noah when she decided to construct Moses' ark. In any case, she—the woman, a slave estranged in a foreign land—built it. She did not plead weakness, cower to intimidation, or deny personal responsibility. She knew falling prey to any of those attitudes would allow her child to fall prey to Pharaoh. So, she did what she could with what was in her hand.

Accepting personal responsibility for decision-making, taking action, and bearing the consequential outcomes under challenging situations and circumstances is a necessary thing. But it can be a hard thing. Some have made honest mistakes, paying a heavy, incongruent price for them at times, breeding deep fears of making another. In my life, having grown up under what I perceived as constant criticism and emotional punishment for mistakes made, I was one of those people. For many years I was immobilized from being able to make decisions for fear of punishment. I couldn't bear the pointed finger of blame that wagged in my mind's eye, torturing my immature heart and mind night and day.

For years into adulthood, in situations that required me to make a choice, I would stall until someone else made the decision. I became perpetually angry—mostly at me, but at them, too. I could not figure out how to unravel the equation and relieve my anguish. Then, one day, sitting in a counselor's office seeking help for a severe eating disorder, I was asked to consider something.

"Kim, I want you to try something on for size. If it doesn't fit you, we will look elsewhere," the counselor said. I agreed to ponder what would come next. "You pretend to be a victim so that you don't have to make decisions for yourself and risk making mistakes. When those decisions don't turn out well, you are angry, but the payoff is that you can blame someone else. You refuse to take personal responsibility for the choices and direction of your life, but you don't like the direction it is going or the decisions being made for you. You are a smart girl capable of making good decisions, but your fear of making a mistake is what is making you sick." I was stunned at first, and then the dam broke. I cried for three weeks as God healed and rebuilt my heart from the inside out.

Like one in every three women, I, too, had been victimized as a little girl and later as a teen. Please don't misunderstand. Neither my counselor nor I would invalidate the pain and suffering of those experiences. Instead, in the tenderness and loving-kindness of the Father, we would grieve with you for what was stolen, agree with you that it is wrong, sinful, and evil, and ask for God to heal your heart, mind, soul, and body.

My counselor was not addressing the experience of being victimized. She was pointing out a disabling way of thinking that was robbing me of the ability to appropriate the power, courage, and authority God had instilled in me. To heal, I had to allow God to expose the truth about my avoidance, the associated fear, and the effect it had on my physical body and emotional stability. His loving-kindness, free of punishment, then set me free. God does not punish us for mistakes; He adjusts them to fit His plan of redemption for our lives. In finding our voice again, our muchness, and in knowing how to possess the strength that God has given to us, we make it clear to the enemy that all the evils done to us do not define us, do not give us our name. We are who God calls us to be, revealed in what we do in God's name—not what others have done to us.

In finding our *muchness*, we are enabled by the power of the Spirit to accept our responsibility in difficult situations and circumstances. We can make choices and take action in response to events, good and bad, in our lives. Those choices and actions will be aligned with our good God and His way of being in creation with His creatures.

God has a plan and a purpose for us, but this never excuses us from participation; rather, it makes us responsible for choosing and acting faithfully. The responsibility to choose and act faithfully is not only for us or even our families, to whom we have responsibilities, especially as parents. It is also for the community. The story Jesus tells in the gospel of Luke that we know as the story of the "Good Samaritan" illustrates our responsibility to see ourselves as a neighbor to all we encounter, embodying the nature and character of Jesus in and to the world.

Let Go

The Midrash recounts how Jochebed lovingly and achingly must have built the ark for her son. A Midrash is an ancient Jewish tool of interpretation or commentary on the Hebrew Scriptures.[23] Often the Midrash is written like a parable.

> Another midrash has Jochebed building a little canopy for Moses inside the ark, for she said to herself: Perhaps I will not see him under his wedding canopy (BT Sotah 12a–b). This portrayal emphasizes the painstaking attention that Jochebed paid to every detail in the ark.[24]

The ark was ready. I wonder if her heart felt ready when she took the ark, took her small son, and placed him inside. She would now do a very hard thing. She would carry out the order of Pharaoh and put her son in the river. It is ironic—the carrying out of the death decree to save his life. Still, as a mother who has felt the warmth of a child in my arms, the resonance of a tiny heartbeat against mine, I can hardly bear the excruciating intensity of her desperate actions. Like the Midrash, we imagine her rehearsing in her heart the milestone events in the life of a child she may never witness: first tooth, first steps, first day at school, first baseball game, first date, weddings and graduations, conversations and meals. Every dream she may have had for him must have rushed through her mind as she loosened her grip on each, one by one.

Rushing into her mind, as well, must have been the uncertainty of the outcome of her actions. Would the ark buoy his life to safety? Would it be strong enough? Could it stay nestled among the reeds on the banks, allowing her to come and go and care for him a while longer? Would he wail and be discovered, only to be ripped from his shelter and thrown into the sea? All these questions and more that we cannot know would only be answered after doing the hardest thing.

She has done all she could do. A shift has come. The time has changed. As the preacher in Ecclesiastes tells us, there is "a time to keep, and a time to cast away."[25] Fear lies to us and causes us to incorrectly hear the truth when it is spoken, telling us there is never a time to let go, never a time to lose control, never a time to stop hoarding, or never a time to stop clinging to what we think is ours. "Take what you can get and take all you can," fear screams at us. Yet, our Father gives. He loved all that He created so unfathomably, so profoundly, and so deeply that He gave His one and only Son for our salvation.

Jochebed had done what was in her hands to do, the only thing she knew to do. Now she must participate differently. Now she must put her work away and, with her own hands, put her God-given reward in the ark, in the Nile, and let go. If she had tightened her grip for a moment instead of opening her hands and letting go of control over what she had given birth to, salvation might never have come. Not for Moses, not for her other children, not for her, not for Israel. Her letting go for the sake of his salvation incarnates her *muchness*.

The agony she must have borne as she laid her innocent, vulnerable, dependent three-month-old infant down, placed the ark on the banks of the Nile, and let it go. Miriam, her daughter who was about a decade or so older than Moses, stood "at a distance to know what would be done to him."[26] Scripture highlights that something was about to be done to him outside his mother's control. Yet, nothing was ever outside of his Father's providential care. Jochebed now entrusts the destiny of her baby boy to God.

Let Go of More

In five short verses following Jochebed placing the ark on the banks of the Nile, we are given the story's climax and its outcome. The sixth verse will jump to, "One day, when Moses had grown up."[27] The deliverer is delivered into the hands of Pharaoh's daughter to live and be adopted into the household of the one who wanted him dead. God is so clever. Girls thwart Pharaoh, who discounted girls from the beginning. Pharaoh, who thought he was a god, is no god compared to the one true God, as God positions the deliverer of Israel—the people Pharaoh won't let go of—in Pharaoh's own house to be fed, clothed, trained, and educated. God left nothing to mere chance. Not even His choice of the midwives, Jochebed, and Pharaoh's daughter as the deliverer's deliverers.

But our story of the muchness of Jochebed is not finished. Listen closely, as a woman yourself, to the last five verses (emphasis mine).

> Now the daughter of Pharaoh came down to bathe at the river. . . . She saw the basket among the reeds and sent her servant woman, and she took it. When she opened it, she saw the child, and behold, the baby was crying. She took pity on him and said, "This is one of the Hebrews' children." Then his sister said to Pharaoh's daughter, "Shall I go and call you a nurse from the Hebrew women to nurse the child for you?" And Pharaoh's daughter said to her, "Go." So the girl went and called the child's mother. And Pharaoh's daughter said to her, "Take this child away and nurse him for me, and I will give you your wages." So the woman took the child and nursed him. When the child grew older, she brought him to Pharaoh's daughter, and *he became her son.*[28]

Salvation has come. It is a cause for celebration, and this child Jochebed has given birth to is now safely in the arms of someone who can rescue him forever from Pharaoh's murder plot. It is joyful. And it is excruciating. Jochebed's child, the life *she* gave birth to, is in the arms of *another woman.* Her child will live, but in another's household under another name, under another *mother.* He will not die, but her dream of mothering her son would. Pharaoh's decree of death killed her dream of raising the life she gave birth to.

Beyond this, which could easily be missed if you read too quickly, Jochebed is called, commanded, and paid wages for nursing her child at her own swollen breasts full of the milk created by his body forming in hers. As the text plainly says, she is no longer the child's mother; she is once again *the unnamed woman*—the slave woman—the child's and his mother's hired servant. In a year or two or three, Jochebed would again lay her child down, this time in a palace, and let go. And she did. The *muchness* of this woman to let go at this depth takes my breath away.

Her letting go facilitated God's purposes to educate Moses in the ways of the Egyptians, to become skilled, strong, and protected until the time of fulfillment of his calling; however, I cannot stress enough that though God had a purpose in it all, she could not have known it at the time. She was not shielded from the pain. Yet, in her pain, she chose to let go.

Do not misunderstand here; she was not casting off the restraint of responsibility. She was not throwing away, cutting her losses, and walking away. She was opening her hand and relinquishing her right to a title, her need to control, and her desire to lead. She would still lead, from behind, from underneath. She let go of any notion of grandiosity to accept obscurity. She let go of any proud, self-centered ambition to humble herself as a servant for the sake of the life of another. And it sets the stage for divinely appointed deliverance to grow up unhindered. Although she did not realize it, her selfless acts were for the sake of the world as she knew it. She did hard things.

Like Jochebed, godly women throughout Israel's history—into and after the life of Jesus—did this hard thing of letting go. Mary, the mother of Jesus, let go of her childhood, reputation, and secured future to say, "Behold, I am the servant of the Lord; let it be to me according to your word."[29] She let go again as her Son was maligned, misunderstood, and sentenced to death, having been foretold, "Behold, this child is appointed for the fall and rising of many in Israel, and for a sign that is opposed (and a sword will pierce through your own soul also), so that thoughts from many hearts may be revealed."[30] How her heart must have been pierced as she stood at the foot of the cross witnessing the death of the Son given her by the Holy Spirit.

She had pondered much in her heart of the mystery of the God-man who was her Son. She could not have known all the purposes of God as she suffered with open hands, but we find her most precious act of letting go as she is counted among the disciples awaiting the gift of the Father on the Day of Pentecost.[31] She stooped down to become her Son's servant and call Him Lord. *Muchness.*

We could speak of Mary Magdalene, who loved Jesus and longed to cling to Him when she found Him in the Garden after His resurrection. "Jesus said to her, 'Do not cling to me, for I have not yet ascended to the Father; but go to my brothers'. . . . Mary Magdalene went and announced to the disciples, 'I have seen the Lord.'"[32] Her courage to let go of the past and her need to cling to a former way of knowing allowed her to step into the fullness of the call on her life.

Letting go requires *muchness*—the courage to entrust into God's hands what you give birth to and the humility to serve when you thought you would lead. It requires being self-sacrificing, self-giving, and selfless when you want to cling, grab, be counted, be acknowledged, and climb the ladder of worldly success. Letting go requires the courage to live openhandedly—without strings attached—regarding all the Lord has given us. Yes, it requires muchness—incredible courage and deep, abiding faith in the God who can keep whatever we entrust to Him so that nothing good is ever lost, even if we have to let loose of it for a time.

Let Go for More

The music was soft and sweet during that morning's chapel worship for all the Master of Divinity students. No one was singing because the atmosphere had become pregnant with something otherworldly, someone Other. I could sense the presence of our holy God. As I raised my hands in worship, a still, small voice broke into the silence of my mind. *You've made an idol of your calling.* The whisper was so kind that it broke my bones. I fell to my face on the ground weeping uncontrollably. I knew it was true, and grief flooded my heart.

After grief, the horror came in a second wave, drenching me in pain and sorrow. I started whispering through the tears, "I'm so sorry. How did this happen? I love You. I didn't even know. How could this happen without my knowing, sensing, seeing it?" To have made an idol of my calling meant that, on the throne of my heart, I had replaced God with what I felt called to do for Him. And I hadn't known it was happening. I didn't know it had happened. It had been a subtle exchange.

There was no condemnation, no shame, and no hint of disappointment from the Lord. Only a radical kindness that continued to overwhelm my heart. It is Isaiah the prophet who prophesies:

> Fear not, for I have redeemed you; I have called you by name, you are mine. When you pass through the waters, I will be with you; and through the rivers, they shall not overwhelm you; when you walk through fire you shall not be burned, and the flame shall not consume you.[33]

This passage is spoken to Israel during their exile. God assures them that whatever trials they face, He will be with them to redeem them. Even though I knew this promise, my situation still felt like a flood of hard truth and a fire of testing. He was calling me not to be afraid to face it because He wanted to heal it—heal me.

My mind began to sift through the last few years until I came to it. I had felt "called" several years earlier to lead a particular ministry. Permission to begin was granted by the senior pastor, so I began. The ministry was starting to flourish when suddenly it was decided someone more qualified (male) should be in the lead. Without further ado, what I had built was given into the hands of another. Naturally, I was hurt and angry. In time, I forgave and healed, or so I thought.

You see, somewhere along the way, in my hurt and anger, I had decided I could not trust anyone with what I felt the Lord had spoken to me. They did not believe it. They did not permit me to do it. So, I decided I had to be the one to protect and defend *my* calling. This is when the thing I called "calling" became an idol in my heart. It was not mine; it never had been. Because it did not belong to me, it was not mine to defend or protect. I knew I had to let go. I had to let go without any strings attached. I had to learn, all over again, to hold the gifts and calling of God with an open hand. I had to relinquish any right to a title, to control, or to a desire to lead. It was a hard thing.

But, like Jochebed and the two Marys, God was working in me for something more, *much more*. These women who courageously let go received back what they had let go of in different forms. Jochebed's story of letting go finds its finale in the Midrash that suggests Jochebed lived long enough to follow her son out of Egypt, witness the leadership of her three children, and enter the land of Canaan, the land of promise.[34] Like Mary after her, Jochebed was found among those following the Lord, led by her son.

Jochebed let go of her son and received a deliverer, who delivered her from Egypt. Mary, the mother of Jesus, let go of a Son and received a Messiah, who gifted her with salvation and the

Holy Spirit at Pentecost. Mary Magdalene let go of her friend and rabbi and received her Savior, the Holy Spirit, and an apostolic calling. I let go of an idol and received the fullness of the call to preach the Gospel in all the world with signs, wonders, and miracles following.

Oh yes, girl, you *can* do hard things. Even the hardest things. Nothing is too hard for God. *Let go.* Let God.

7

Defy the Religious Spirit

THE STORY OF THE SINNER OF THE CITY

· LUKE 7:36–50 ·

I once was lost, but now I'm found, was blind but now I see.[1]

*Y*OU KNOW, *there is a worship that defies the religious spirit.*

The tone was a matter-of-fact, just thrown out casually, even dispassionate, withheld till just the right moment to maximize the effect. A one-liner that assumes a whole conversation you ought to know but never had, causing you to jerk your head up.

It worked. I jerked my head up. It was not audible, but clear in my heart and mind. Whether it was the Spirit or my spirit,

I cannot guarantee. I am convinced He speaks, and I confess it is my persistent endeavor to be available to the mystery of God speaking to His creatures. So, I listen the best I can, admitting imperfection at best and blunder at worst. There are, however, moments when words have come to my heart and mind that have been His, and they changed my life—and sometimes, the lives of others.

Anyhow, I *knew* that the story in Luke of the woman who was a sinner with her *me'od*—her *muchness*—was the key to unlocking the interpretation of the phrase I had heard.[2] It is how I came to love her story. I believe she is every one of us, male and female. She provokes, confronts, and shocks us into a fresh revelation of all we have in Christ. This is her story.

Conflict

Our story is one of several conflict stories in Luke. The conflicts arise with demons, nature, sickness, people, civil authorities, and Israel's religious leaders. This is nothing new, of course. Life is full of conflict. As for demons, this, too, is nothing new. From beginning to end, Genesis to Revelation, the enemy opposes God's will and purpose by any means possible to keep humanity from becoming fully human and fulfilling God's call to faithfully represent Him in the earth.

Conflict stories in the gospels reveal truth about Jesus. In them, Jesus is scandalizing and exposing every cultural and religious expectation of His identity, work, and mission that have been corrupted by systems created by human philosophy and ideology. And precisely for that reason, they also reveal the truth about you and me. The conflict stories are like a mirror by which we are offered a unique opportunity to examine ourselves and reflect on what we see. Sometimes what we think of ourselves is not what we behold in the mirror of Scripture. Jesus described this very human propensity when He said, "If anyone is a hearer of the word and not a doer, he is like a man who looks intently at his natural face in a mirror. For he looks at himself and goes away and at once forgets what he was like."[3]

Scripture's goal, especially in conflict, is to draw us into the story so that we place ourselves in the roles of every character reacting or responding to God. And we are presented with an opportunity to answer the question arising from the story. What is the question in the story we are about to hear? It is this: Do you see?

The Singing Soul

Luke is a masterful storyteller. In his account of "all that Jesus began to do and teach,"[4] he highlights the compassion of Jesus, who goes around healing all that ails us. Perhaps it is because Luke is himself a physician. Throughout Luke's gospel, and immediately before our story, Jesus has been demonstrating the Kingdom and announcing its extraordinarily Good News to the unclean, the outcast, the voiceless, the lost, the broken, the rejected, and the racially, socially, economically, or religiously marginalized. And yes, to the immoral also. They are responding—in droves.

I was thirteen years old when the little Southern Baptist church my family and I attended lost its worship leader. The pastor asked me if I would lead worship. Why he asked me, I do not know; I had not volunteered. In my naivete and innocent arrogance, I gleefully accepted the opportunity to be on stage. I loved Jesus, to be sure, but I also loved performing. Each week, I stood on the small platform behind the pulpit and belted out songs from the hymnal a capella at the top of my lungs (which means very loudly). If nothing else, I had zeal and could stay on pitch.

The memories of that time have faded some but what remains is the indelible mark on my heart made by those songs. To this day, I love hymns. The words came alive in those weeks as I led the congregation. My favorite hymn is "I Surrender All," and to this day, I can barely utter the words without tears falling down my face. Still, it was the most famous hymn worldwide that helped me understand in simple language the wonder of salvation: "Amazing grace, how sweet the sound that saved a wretch like me. I once was lost, but now I'm found, was blind, but now I see."

Something happens when our eyes are opened to the realization of what Christ has done for us. "How Great Thou Art," another world-renowned hymn, says it best. If you have a moment, look up the lyrics online. I love the third verse, where the writer describes meditating on Jesus and His sacrifice. When he thinks on these things, he can't help but burst forth, "Then sings my soul"!

Did you catch it? When we see Jesus, the One who rescues us from sin, bondage, and death and makes all things clean and new, when we perceive His holiness and worthiness in complete contrast to our unworthiness and unholiness, and when we realize that it was all His doing, His plan, His loving-kindness, grace, and greatness, our soul responds by bowing low in worship. When we know that we know that we know that without Him we would still be in our wretchedness and sin, and when we see the One who has done it all for us, we sing the song of the redeemed.

Jesus has conquered darkness, death, and the devil. He heals our diseases and casts out our demons. He is the Light in the dark, the Truth that sets us free (from all deception: self-centered, cultural, demonic), and He points us to a life we have not known but ever yearned to have. He not only removes the barrier between this life and eternity for us but also restores the dignity of the rejected among us, giving them back to the community *and* demonstrating His kindness and hospitality for all. Isn't He wonderful?!

Yes, He is, but *not everyone* is convinced. Why? How can it be that some of us respond in gratitude and awe, as the one leper did, seeing that he had been healed, while others seem not to respond at all?[5] They all had cried out in a loud voice, "Jesus, have mercy on us!" But only one turned back in praise—also in a loud voice. "Where are the other nine?"[6]

Israel's religious leaders are the *not everyone* in Luke's gospel. Not all of them, of course. Every stereotype always has exceptions. Still, for the most part, we are talking about the stereotypical group in our story. Luke recounts, "And the Pharisees and their scribes grumbled at his disciples, saying, 'Why do you eat and drink with tax collectors and sinners?'"[7] Eating and drinking with tax collectors and sinners is a not-so-subtle accusation. They accuse Jesus of being perverted and polluted, unclean or ritually impure, making Him suspect or worse, an unbeliever. Essentially, they say He is a disobedient, unruly Son, resistant to or rebuffing God and His Law, evidenced by His association with those who do likewise.[8] These charges are worthy of being stoned to death.

Further, Jesus is being "rejected for not following the conventions determined and propagated by religious people who claim that those conventions are divinely sanctioned," explains Joel Green.[9] In other words, Jesus is not following the accepted religious agenda established by the religious elites. The ministry of Jesus challenged and turned upside down religious belief systems. It created conflict and polarization, separating and dividing people according to who and what they believed. Many religious leaders were scandalized by it. The people called Jesus a prophet, possibly even the long-awaited Messiah, but according to the religious system, as we call it, He was scandalous and perhaps even blasphemous. They concluded, therefore, that it could not be so. He did not fit the messianic expectations of the time. He was not at all what they expected and, therefore, not at all to be believed.

The religious leaders, at least the loudest ones, were offended. Jesus knew it and told them that the one not offended by Him would come to experience the goodness of God. We must be careful at this point. The moment we are aware of the sins of others, the moment they seem to us as though they are people we could never love, the moment their sins seem worse to us than our own, we have fallen into temptation.

Remember that the disciples, as well as their families, those who loved Jesus and believed in Him, were also offended by much of what Jesus said, did, and failed to say and do. Lest we think we are safe from being offended by Jesus, He didn't only speak to the religious leaders—He spoke to everyone. Even John the Baptist, the great prophet preparing the way of the Lord, was in danger of being offended.

John, like everyone else, expected a revolution when the Messiah came. He expected that Jesus, if He were the *One who was coming,* would set up His Kingdom on earth, overthrowing the sociopolitical oppressors, rebuking and reforming religious corruption, establishing Himself as ruler, and putting Israel back on top. I wonder if he also expected Jesus to intervene on his behalf since he had been imprisoned unjustly. Yet it seemed Jesus was not doing any of what he expected, nor lifting a finger to defend and deliver him. At least not in the way John had expected.

Offense is dangerous because it becomes a stumbling block that leads to unbelief. We are tempted to turn away from faith and Jesus when offense takes root. In *The Way of the Kingdom*, I illustrate how offense works:

> Just this week I read of another worship leader who publicly renounced his faith in God. He is no longer a Christian. What was his reason? He became offended. He asked how a just God could allow injustice. How could a loving God send people to hell? How could a kind God allow people to suffer the horrors of sickness and evil. . . . He became offended at God, and he no longer believes.
>
> Over my years of pastoring, I have counseled many who had become offended at God because of a terrible injustice, a hurtful betrayal or a loved one who had suffered and died a violent death. How often do we, when we have unmet expectations or when we begin to feel the sharp edge of opposition and injustice, become offended with God? We begin to doubt His love, His goodness, His faithfulness, His presence and even His reality. How many have turned back and no longer followed Jesus because of this very thing?
>
> We expected to be treated differently. We expected a circumstance to end differently. We expected God to come through— after all, we believed Him. Can you hear what is happening here? We become the judge who is putting God on trial. We hold God responsible and accountable for our pain and suffering. We hold up our wounds and scars, our failed agendas and unmet expectations, and ask Him to explain Himself. . . . We judge God because we are offended by Him. We are offended that He did not do what we expected Him to do. In our judgments, Jesus comes and says to us . . . "Blessed is the one who is not offended by me."[10]

For each of us, failed expectations and subsequent judgments of Jesus—what we perceive Him to be or not to be doing—can lead to offense. Our fear or pride in moments of intense suffering can deceive us into thinking we know better than God how and when things should have been done. It's a very human response to the human experience. Sometimes, beyond being a very human response, it becomes demonically inspired and driven. The enemy of our soul and his minions delight in stoking the fires of doubt and fear in those created and loved by God. We become blinded and are kept from seeing how God, by His Spirit, in His loving-kindness and mercy, *is* acting on our behalf. Becoming blinded in this way also steals our opportunity to humbly accept His working and embrace His comfort in the wilderness called suffering.

Jesus, unafraid and undisturbed by false accusations or expectations, knows He is upsetting the established, predetermined religious system of the leaders. He answers their charges by exposing their inability to see what God is doing.

> "For John the Baptist has come eating no bread and drinking no wine, and you say, 'He has a demon.' The Son of Man has come eating and drinking, and you say, 'Look at him! A glutton and a drunkard, a friend of tax collectors and sinners!' Yet wisdom is justified by all her children."[11]

They did not accept John, and they did not accept Jesus. They are not wisdom's children. And again, we must stand before this judgment in fear and trembling, remembering that Jesus does not see as we see and does not judge as we judge. "Who is blind but my servant, and deaf as my messenger whom I send?" (Isaiah 42:19). It is precisely for that reason that Jesus is misjudged—by the people who pride themselves on being right, being good, being godly. Those who are sure of their rightness before God and sure that this gives them a right to correct others always end up doing the devil's work for him. Remember Job's friends.

Instead, against all expectations, Jesus is bringing the Kingdom near to the poor, the outcast, and the immoral, healing their bodies and broken hearts, casting out demons to free them from bondage, and showing them, in living demonstration, the mercy and loving-kindness of His Father. It is these, the ones who know they are part of the group labeled "sinners and tax collectors," who are not offended by Him. They are the lost being found. They are the ones coming into the Kingdom of God. They are those who now see. They are the ones whose souls begin to sing.

All of that is easy to say, but hard to see—especially when it is happening in our lives and in the lives of those around us. We have no difficulty celebrating Jesus' friendship with sinners—as long as they remain safely distant from us, bottled up in the stories we're reading, locked away in the past we're studying. We're happy to sing Jesus' praises, but when His troubled and troublesome friends show up on our doorstep, move into our neighborhood, or slide into the seats in our churches, it's hard not to change our tune.

This is where our story within the larger story begins—in the house of a man who cannot see and refuses to sing.

The House of Religious Spirits

> One of the Pharisees asked him to eat with him, and he went into the Pharisee's house and reclined at table.[12]

A dinner invitation seems innocuous—so, well, insignificant. Remembering that this dinner comes on the heels of learning that many religious leaders rejected Jesus—the friend of sinners and tax collectors—and knowing that a Pharisee is a spiritual leader, the invitation becomes curious and even surprising. There must be something more hidden in the story that is to be found like treasure.

In the culture of Israel and the New Testament, a dinner invitation is tantamount to being welcomed to fellowship, even if only for the purpose of a hearing. Conversation, friendly debate, and discussion were part of reclining at table for dinner in the house of a Pharisee. Inviting Jesus to dinner shows a willingness to hear what Jesus has to say and to engage in a friendly debate about His views. Still, a dinner invitation is not the same as a capitulation to faith. More plausible is that the invitation is a way for the Pharisee to see if Jesus is all that the people and He Himself claims that He is. If he exposes Jesus for the fraud others suggest He is, all the better to exalt his reputation among the leaders and the people. Whatever the motive, it seems this Pharisee, whose name is Simon, is open to finding out for himself. The surprise is that not all Pharisees and religious leaders are inexorably committed to opposing Jesus without cause. Already, a religious system is being challenged—our own. Yours and mine.

Meals in every culture are important. The table is a place of meeting and sharing as friends and family, it is a place of healing, discovery, and, yes, it is a place of communion, in which we discover that we belong. It can be a place of illumination, redemption, and restoration when Jesus is at the table.

Jesus is ever ready and willing to come in and dine wherever He is invited—to the house of any who are curious, doubting, vetting, or believing. He comes to all, both sinner and saint, with arms wide open, unafraid to answer the questions of our hearts with His love. He is the God who makes the sun shine and the rains fall on both the evil and the good, for He is no respecter of persons, shows no partiality, and yearns for all to be saved and none to perish.[13] Jesus goes to Simon's house and sits at his table. Simon is the one who invited Jesus to dinner, but it will be Jesus who sets the table in the presence of those who are at this time His enemies, hoping that they will become His friends.

So, Jesus is invited to dinner, reclines at the table, and immediately, without any preparation, *behold*, there is drama. The text screams at us to wake up and pay undivided, undistracted attention because something extraordinary is happening. "And *behold*," reads the Scripture. See, the word *behold* is no mere verb. It means for us to look and see something. It is a *marker* that "livens up" the narrative, emphasizing some detail in the story.[14]

We already know Jesus is bringing in the Kingdom of God in unexpected ways. Or at least, we know that we're supposed to know that. He is breaking with socio-religious convention, as He always does. He is upending traditions that have become whole systems—ideologies—that have created and established unjust measurements and standards for who is in and who is out, who deserves honor and who does not, who is to be seen and heard and who is not. It can happen in any group of people, society, or culture. Hospitality becomes limited to those who measure up to the standard. Those who do not are judged as below standard, indicted and outcast, dismissed, not to be named aloud, and finally unseen.

Haven't we all been victims of such measurements at some time or another? Sometimes we were the ones judged, and sometimes we were the ones who judged. Either way, the judgments used measures and standards meant to discover defects to dismiss or degrade. It is especially tragic when it happens in the Church. But when it does, it clearly indicates a religious spirit.

In many Pentecostal and charismatic circles, a religious spirit is a demon, an evil spirit. This is a commonly held view. Time and space do not allow me to explain all the details of spiritual warfare in the cosmos; however, demons are attested to in Scripture. I also want to point out that neither Satan nor his demons are equal to God. They are forever conquered and under judgment by the finished work of Christ on the cross. And they are subject to us by the power of both the name of Jesus and His Holy Spirit as we abide in Christ through faith.[15] We need not fear.

Whatever else it or they may do, religious spirits instigate a corrupted system of religious belief through human cooperation, resulting in a particular pattern of behavior that undermines and even forbids the kind of hospitality modeled by Jesus. In this way, the Church can become a house of religious spirits that do not see and cannot sing. The people have become too busy critiquing—and, in effect, cursing—those they believe are blind and joyless.

The Woman Who Was a Sinner

> And behold, a woman of the city, who was a sinner, when she learned that he was reclining at table in the Pharisee's house, brought an alabaster flask of ointment, and standing behind him at his feet, weeping, she began to wet his feet with her tears and wiped them with the hair of her head and kissed his feet and anointed them with the ointment.[16]

What was the extraordinary thing happening to which we were supposed to pay such close attention? A woman. A woman who has no name but has a designation, categorization, and reputation that precedes her. She is an uninvited guest, a nobody that nobody would want to associate with unless it were of a sordid

nature. The only remarkable thing about her is that she is a sinner, and everyone seems to know it. She, too, knows it.

Again, what is the extraordinary thing we must pay undistracted attention to? A woman of the city who was a sinner, most likely a prostitute, who bursts into the room, into Simon's house. Simon the Pharisee is a man with a name. He, too, has a designation, categorization, and reputation to protect. Unlike Jesus, he has made of himself a reputation. He has worked hard to achieve his social and religious standing, a treasured and honored guest at every banquet. He is somebody who everybody would want to associate with to be judged a saint. How many men of good standing and status, like Simon or those reclining at his table, took advantage of women like her in the dark behind closed doors without ever incurring the slightest damage to their pristine reputations? We do not know.

We know that this woman brazenly and unpredictably interrupts the dinner designed by Simon to test this Jesus who was said to be a prophet. She becomes the test. There will be no need for discussion and debate over ancient writings and interpretations. If Jesus is a prophet, Simon reasons, He will see and discern (prophetically perceive) what this woman is. After all, Simon knows what she is. She is *hamartia*—a sinner, a lost cause—sullied, compromised, tainted, stained, immoral, unworthy, unclean, unseen, and unnamed.[17] She has no identity, community, compassion, or mercy among the religious.

She doesn't care. She heard *He* was at Simon's house. *Jesus* was there! The semantics reveal a prior encounter between Jesus and the woman, but we have no other details about it. Instead, as is so often the case for any who experience the love of God in Christ Jesus, we see the dramatic aftermath of their encounter. The text is silent on the matter, but I wonder if she had a plan

about what she would do when she got to Him. The ointment is expensive, even extravagant. It would have cost her much. In her line of business, we can only imagine that cost. It seems that what she had been given by Him when they met drove her to look for something to give Him in return. Precious for precious, perhaps knowing it wouldn't be enough. She *had* to worship Him. She *had* to do something to honor Him. She takes us with her into this unfolding holy drama. We scarcely can think or breathe.

When she gets close, it seems she cannot hold back the torrent of gratitude and love. The urgency in her worship of Jesus is arresting, causing our hearts to quicken. We are suddenly swept up in the moment with her. We are there with her at His feet, the feet of Jesus. She was driven, compelled, wholly abandoned. She throws herself at His feet in sheer beauty and sacred vulnerability, as though she can't get low enough before Him. The worship she offers is so extravagant, so exquisitely intimate that it is nearly embarrassing to witness. The gift she brought is not what was in the jar. She brought herself. She offered herself in worship at His feet.

We are left asking, What could be her motive? We will soon enough find out. We are now witnessing a woman caught up in worship, oblivious to social customs, with invulnerability to the fear of being judged or put to shame. After all, perfect love casts out fear.

This beautiful scene is being played out in the house of religious spirits, in a religious system inhospitable to those who do not measure up to the conventional standards. Because the woman of the city was a sinner, her offering is misjudged, mischaracterized, and misunderstood.

Perhaps it is because she has long been invisible in her community, or maybe it was because of her line of business, but she has

Though a spiritual leader of the people who was known for the strictness of purity and holiness down to the smallest letter of the Law, he and others like him had "neglected the weightier matters of the law: justice and mercy and faithfulness," making them blind and unfit to lead people out of slavery into the promised goodness of God.[21]

Jesus is showing Simon, in His mercy and kindness, that he does not *see* beyond his judgments. "Simon, do you see this woman?" Jesus asks. Jesus knows Simon only sees a sinner acting sinfully. He does not *see* the woman. He does not *see* Jesus. The evidence is in Simon's lack of hospitality to both Jesus and the woman. Now Jesus is going to help Simon open his eyes to the something more before him.

> "Do you see this woman? I entered your house; you gave me no water for my feet, but she has wet my feet with her tears and wiped them with her hair. You gave me no kiss, but from the time I came in she has not ceased to kiss my feet. You did not anoint my head with oil, but she has anointed my feet with ointment. Therefore I tell you, her sins, which are many, are forgiven—for she loved much. But he who is forgiven little, loves little." And he said to her, "Your sins are forgiven."[22]

Forgiveness. This is the reason she worshiped. Unlike Simon, she knew she was a sinner. When her many sins were forgiven, her love, fueled by gratitude, overwhelmed any consideration of social or religious convention. She was a sinner saved by the grace of God. Her shame was gone, and though once a prostitute, she gave herself to Jesus in a physical expression of love and gratitude that, though misinterpreted by those around her, was innocent of sensual seduction, cleansed from the manipulation, exploitation, and abuse of her body by herself and others. She was free.

The Pharisee was not willing to do what the prostitute was desperate to do—prove her love. He did not see a need to. He had nothing to be grateful to Jesus for. He had invited Jesus to his house to test Him, not to serve Him. Simon served the system. Or more to the point, the system used Simon.

We can become so blind when we think we are serving God by following the predetermined conventions of a system created by religious spirits and blind guides. Religious spirits tell us our religious works are a testimony to our righteousness. Simon was blind to his own need for Jesus. He loved little, not seeing the enormous debt that he owed. Jesus—the Messiah—was in his house, but he did not bow in worship; his soul did not sing.

His religious spirit had deceived him into thinking he was superior. United with self-righteousness, he judged the woman a sinner and Jesus as a fraud, and he could not see his way to consider and judge his own sin. Even still, Jesus had come to sit at his table and hold out an opportunity for something more; healing for his blindness. Simon was blind to his need for a savior—for the Savior right in front of him. He did not know he was in the very presence of God.

The Worship That Defies a Religious Spirit

Then those who were at table with him began to say among themselves, "Who is this, who even forgives sins?"[23]

And with this question, from those at the table in the house of religious spirits, we find ourselves back at the beginning, full circle. Our story is about an unnamed woman (why, we should ask, does the Spirit keep her name from us?), caught in conflict with a religious system created by those who suppose themselves

Though a spiritual leader of the people who was known for the strictness of purity and holiness down to the smallest letter of the Law, he and others like him had "neglected the weightier matters of the law: justice and mercy and faithfulness," making them blind and unfit to lead people out of slavery into the promised goodness of God.[21]

Jesus is showing Simon, in His mercy and kindness, that he does not *see* beyond his judgments. "Simon, do you see this woman?" Jesus asks. Jesus knows Simon only sees a sinner acting sinfully. He does not *see* the woman. He does not *see* Jesus. The evidence is in Simon's lack of hospitality to both Jesus and the woman. Now Jesus is going to help Simon open his eyes to the something more before him.

> "Do you see this woman? I entered your house; you gave me no water for my feet, but she has wet my feet with her tears and wiped them with her hair. You gave me no kiss, but from the time I came in she has not ceased to kiss my feet. You did not anoint my head with oil, but she has anointed my feet with ointment. Therefore I tell you, her sins, which are many, are forgiven—for she loved much. But he who is forgiven little, loves little." And he said to her, "Your sins are forgiven."[22]

Forgiveness. This is the reason she worshiped. Unlike Simon, she knew she was a sinner. When her many sins were forgiven, her love, fueled by gratitude, overwhelmed any consideration of social or religious convention. She was a sinner saved by the grace of God. Her shame was gone, and though once a prostitute, she gave herself to Jesus in a physical expression of love and gratitude that, though misinterpreted by those around her, was innocent of sensual seduction, cleansed from the manipulation, exploitation, and abuse of her body by herself and others. She was free.

The Pharisee was not willing to do what the prostitu[...] desperate to do—prove her love. He did not see a need [...] had nothing to be grateful to Jesus for. He had invited Jesus [...] house to test Him, not to serve Him. Simon served the s[...] Or more to the point, the system used Simon.

We can become so blind when we think we are servin[...] by following the predetermined conventions of a system c[...] by religious spirits and blind guides. Religious spirits tell [...] religious works are a testimony to our righteousness. Simo[...] blind to his own need for Jesus. He loved little, not seei[...] enormous debt that he owed. Jesus—the Messiah—was [...] house, but he did not bow in worship; his soul did not sin[...]

His religious spirit had deceived him into thinking h[...] superior. United with self-righteousness, he judged the wo[...] sinner and Jesus as a fraud, and he could not see his way to[...] sider and judge his own sin. Even still, Jesus had come to sit [...] table and hold out an opportunity for something more; he[...] for his blindness. Simon was blind to his need for a savior[...] the Savior right in front of him. He did not know he was i[...] very presence of God.

The Worship That Defies a Religious Spirit

Then those who were at table with him began to say among the[...] selves, "Who is this, who even forgives sins?"[23]

And with this question, from those at the table in the hou[...] religious spirits, we find ourselves back at the beginning[...] circle. Our story is about an unnamed woman (why, we sh[...] ask, does the Spirit keep her name from us?), caught in co[...] with a religious system created by those who suppose thems[...]

Though a spiritual leader of the people who was known for the strictness of purity and holiness down to the smallest letter of the Law, he and others like him had "neglected the weightier matters of the law: justice and mercy and faithfulness," making them blind and unfit to lead people out of slavery into the promised goodness of God.[21]

Jesus is showing Simon, in His mercy and kindness, that he does not *see* beyond his judgments. "Simon, do you see this woman?" Jesus asks. Jesus knows Simon only sees a sinner acting sinfully. He does not *see* the woman. He does not *see* Jesus. The evidence is in Simon's lack of hospitality to both Jesus and the woman. Now Jesus is going to help Simon open his eyes to the something more before him.

> "Do you see this woman? I entered your house; you gave me no water for my feet, but she has wet my feet with her tears and wiped them with her hair. You gave me no kiss, but from the time I came in she has not ceased to kiss my feet. You did not anoint my head with oil, but she has anointed my feet with ointment. Therefore I tell you, her sins, which are many, are forgiven—for she loved much. But he who is forgiven little, loves little." And he said to her, "Your sins are forgiven."[22]

Forgiveness. This is the reason she worshiped. Unlike Simon, she knew she was a sinner. When her many sins were forgiven, her love, fueled by gratitude, overwhelmed any consideration of social or religious convention. She was a sinner saved by the grace of God. Her shame was gone, and though once a prostitute, she gave herself to Jesus in a physical expression of love and gratitude that, though misinterpreted by those around her, was innocent of sensual seduction, cleansed from the manipulation, exploitation, and abuse of her body by herself and others. She was free.

165

The Pharisee was not willing to do what the prostitute was desperate to do—prove her love. He did not see a need. He had nothing to be grateful to Jesus for. He had invited Jesus into His house to test Him, not to serve Him. Simon served the system. Or more to the point, the system used Simon.

We can become so blind when we think we are serving God by following the predetermined conventions of a system created by religious spirits and blind guides. Religious spirits tell us our religious works are a testimony to our righteousness. Simon was blind to his own need for Jesus. He loved little, not seeing the enormous debt that he owed. Jesus—the Messiah—was in his house, but he did not bow in worship; his soul did not sing.

His religious spirit had deceived him into thinking he was superior. United with self-righteousness, he judged the woman as sinner and Jesus as a fraud, and he could not see his way to consider and judge his own sin. Even still, Jesus had come to sit at his table and hold out an opportunity for something more; healing for his blindness. Simon was blind to his need for a savior and the Savior right in front of him. He did not know he was in the very presence of God.

The Worship That Defies a Religious Spirit

> Then those who were at table with him began to say among themselves, "Who is this, who even forgives sins?"[23]

And with this question, from those at the table in the house of religious spirits, we find ourselves back at the beginning, full circle. Our story is about an unnamed woman (why, we should ask, does the Spirit keep her name from us?), caught in conflict with a religious system created by those who suppose themselves

Though a spiritual leader of the people who was known for the strictness of purity and holiness down to the smallest letter of the Law, he and others like him had "neglected the weightier matters of the law: justice and mercy and faithfulness," making them blind and unfit to lead people out of slavery into the promised goodness of God.[21]

Jesus is showing Simon, in His mercy and kindness, that he does not *see* beyond his judgments. "Simon, do you see this woman?" Jesus asks. Jesus knows Simon only sees a sinner acting sinfully. He does not *see* the woman. He does not *see* Jesus. The evidence is in Simon's lack of hospitality to both Jesus and the woman. Now Jesus is going to help Simon open his eyes to the something more before him.

> "Do you see this woman? I entered your house; you gave me no water for my feet, but she has wet my feet with her tears and wiped them with her hair. You gave me no kiss, but from the time I came in she has not ceased to kiss my feet. You did not anoint my head with oil, but she has anointed my feet with ointment. Therefore I tell you, her sins, which are many, are forgiven—for she loved much. But he who is forgiven little, loves little." And he said to her, "Your sins are forgiven."[22]

Forgiveness. This is the reason she worshiped. Unlike Simon, she knew she was a sinner. When her many sins were forgiven, her love, fueled by gratitude, overwhelmed any consideration of social or religious convention. She was a sinner saved by the grace of God. Her shame was gone, and though once a prostitute, she gave herself to Jesus in a physical expression of love and gratitude that, though misinterpreted by those around her, was innocent of sensual seduction, cleansed from the manipulation, exploitation, and abuse of her body by herself and others. She was free.

The Pharisee was not willing to do what the prostitute was desperate to do—prove her love. He did not see a need. He had nothing to be grateful to Jesus for. He had invited Jesus to his house to test Him, not to serve Him. Simon served the system. Or more to the point, the system used Simon.

We can become so blind when we think we are serving God by following the predetermined conventions of a system created by religious spirits and blind guides. Religious spirits tell us our religious works are a testimony to our righteousness. Simon was blind to his own need for Jesus. He loved little, not seeing the enormous debt that he owed. Jesus—the Messiah—was in his house, but he did not bow in worship; his soul did not sing.

His religious spirit had deceived him into thinking he was superior. United with self-righteousness, he judged the woman a sinner and Jesus as a fraud, and he could not see his way to consider and judge his own sin. Even still, Jesus had come to sit at his table and hold out an opportunity for something more; healing for his blindness. Simon was blind to his need for a savior—for the Savior right in front of him. He did not know he was in the very presence of God.

The Worship That Defies a Religious Spirit

> Then those who were at table with him began to say among themselves, "Who is this, who even forgives sins?"[23]

And with this question, from those at the table in the house of religious spirits, we find ourselves back at the beginning, full circle. Our story is about an unnamed woman (why, we should ask, does the Spirit keep her name from us?), caught in conflict with a religious system created by those who suppose themselves

Though a spiritual leader of the people who was known for the strictness of purity and holiness down to the smallest letter of the Law, he and others like him had "neglected the weightier matters of the law: justice and mercy and faithfulness," making them blind and unfit to lead people out of slavery into the promised goodness of God.[21]

Jesus is showing Simon, in His mercy and kindness, that he does not *see* beyond his judgments. "Simon, do you see this woman?" Jesus asks. Jesus knows Simon only sees a sinner acting sinfully. He does not *see* the woman. He does not *see* Jesus. The evidence is in Simon's lack of hospitality to both Jesus and the woman. Now Jesus is going to help Simon open his eyes to the something more before him.

> "Do you see this woman? I entered your house; you gave me no water for my feet, but she has wet my feet with her tears and wiped them with her hair. You gave me no kiss, but from the time I came in she has not ceased to kiss my feet. You did not anoint my head with oil, but she has anointed my feet with ointment. Therefore I tell you, her sins, which are many, are forgiven—for she loved much. But he who is forgiven little, loves little." And he said to her, "Your sins are forgiven."[22]

Forgiveness. This is the reason she worshiped. Unlike Simon, she knew she was a sinner. When her many sins were forgiven, her love, fueled by gratitude, overwhelmed any consideration of social or religious convention. She was a sinner saved by the grace of God. Her shame was gone, and though once a prostitute, she gave herself to Jesus in a physical expression of love and gratitude that, though misinterpreted by those around her, was innocent of sensual seduction, cleansed from the manipulation, exploitation, and abuse of her body by herself and others. She was free.

The Pharisee was not willing to do what the prostitute was desperate to do—prove her love. He did not see a need to had nothing to be grateful to Jesus for. He had invited Jesus to house to test Him, not to serve Him. Simon served the system. Or more to the point, the system used Simon.

We can become so blind when we think we are serving by following the predetermined conventions of a system created by religious spirits and blind guides. Religious spirits tell us our religious works are a testimony to our righteousness. Simon was blind to his own need for Jesus. He loved little, not seeing the enormous debt that he owed. Jesus—the Messiah—was in his house, but he did not bow in worship; his soul did not sing.

His religious spirit had deceived him into thinking he was superior. United with self-righteousness, he judged the woman a sinner and Jesus as a fraud, and he could not see his way to consider and judge his own sin. Even still, Jesus had come to sit at his table and hold out an opportunity for something more; healing for his blindness. Simon was blind to his need for a savior—for the Savior right in front of him. He did not know he was in the very presence of God.

The Worship That Defies a Religious Spirit

> Then those who were at table with him began to say among themselves, "Who is this, who even forgives sins?"[23]

And with this question, from those at the table in the house of religious spirits, we find ourselves back at the beginning, full circle. Our story is about an unnamed woman (why, we should ask, does the Spirit keep her name from us?), caught in conflict with a religious system created by those who suppose themselves

nature. The only remarkable thing about her is that she is a sinner, and everyone seems to know it. She, too, knows it.

Again, what is the extraordinary thing we must pay undistracted attention to? A woman of the city who was a sinner, most likely a prostitute, who bursts into the room, into Simon's house. Simon the Pharisee is a man with a name. He, too, has a designation, categorization, and reputation to protect. Unlike Jesus, he has made of himself a reputation. He has worked hard to achieve his social and religious standing, a treasured and honored guest at every banquet. He is somebody who everybody would want to associate with to be judged a saint. How many men of good standing and status, like Simon or those reclining at his table, took advantage of women like her in the dark behind closed doors without ever incurring the slightest damage to their pristine reputations? We do not know.

We know that this woman brazenly and unpredictably interrupts the dinner designed by Simon to test this Jesus who was said to be a prophet. She becomes the test. There will be no need for discussion and debate over ancient writings and interpretations. If Jesus is a prophet, Simon reasons, He will see and discern (prophetically perceive) what this woman is. After all, Simon knows what she is. She is *hamartia*—a sinner, a lost cause—sullied, compromised, tainted, stained, immoral, unworthy, unclean, unseen, and unnamed.[17] She has no identity, community, compassion, or mercy among the religious.

She doesn't care. She heard *He* was at Simon's house. *Jesus* was there! The semantics reveal a prior encounter between Jesus and the woman, but we have no other details about it. Instead, as is so often the case for any who experience the love of God in Christ Jesus, we see the dramatic aftermath of their encounter. The text is silent on the matter, but I wonder if she had a plan

about what she would do when she got to Him. The ointment is expensive, even extravagant. It would have cost her much. In her line of business, we can only imagine that cost. It seems that what she had been given by Him when they met drove her to look for something to give Him in return. Precious for precious, perhaps knowing it wouldn't be enough. She *had* to worship Him. She *had* to do something to honor Him. She takes us with her into this unfolding holy drama. We scarcely can think or breathe.

When she gets close, it seems she cannot hold back the torrent of gratitude and love. The urgency in her worship of Jesus is arresting, causing our hearts to quicken. We are suddenly swept up in the moment with her. We are there with her at His feet, the feet of Jesus. She was driven, compelled, wholly abandoned. She throws herself at His feet in sheer beauty and sacred vulnerability, as though she can't get low enough before Him. The worship she offers is so extravagant, so exquisitely intimate that it is nearly embarrassing to witness. The gift she brought is not what was in the jar. She brought herself. She offered herself in worship at His feet.

We are left asking, What could be her motive? We will soon enough find out. We are now witnessing a woman caught up in worship, oblivious to social customs, with invulnerability to the fear of being judged or put to shame. After all, perfect love casts out fear.

This beautiful scene is being played out in the house of religious spirits, in a religious system inhospitable to those who do not measure up to the conventional standards. Because the woman of the city was a sinner, her offering is misjudged, mischaracterized, and misunderstood.

Perhaps it is because she has long been invisible in her community, or maybe it was because of her line of business, but she has

nature. The only remarkable thing about her is that she is a sinner, and everyone seems to know it. She, too, knows it.

Again, what is the extraordinary thing we must pay undistracted attention to? A woman of the city who was a sinner, most likely a prostitute, who bursts into the room, into Simon's house. Simon the Pharisee is a man with a name. He, too, has a designation, categorization, and reputation to protect. Unlike Jesus, he has made of himself a reputation. He has worked hard to achieve his social and religious standing, a treasured and honored guest at every banquet. He is somebody who everybody would want to associate with to be judged a saint. How many men of good standing and status, like Simon or those reclining at his table, took advantage of women like her in the dark behind closed doors without ever incurring the slightest damage to their pristine reputations? We do not know.

We know that this woman brazenly and unpredictably interrupts the dinner designed by Simon to test this Jesus who was said to be a prophet. She becomes the test. There will be no need for discussion and debate over ancient writings and interpretations. If Jesus is a prophet, Simon reasons, He will see and discern (prophetically perceive) what this woman is. After all, Simon knows what she is. She is *hamartia*—a sinner, a lost cause—sullied, compromised, tainted, stained, immoral, unworthy, unclean, unseen, and unnamed.[17] She has no identity, community, compassion, or mercy among the religious.

She doesn't care. She heard *He* was at Simon's house. *Jesus* was there! The semantics reveal a prior encounter between Jesus and the woman, but we have no other details about it. Instead, as is so often the case for any who experience the love of God in Christ Jesus, we see the dramatic aftermath of their encounter. The text is silent on the matter, but I wonder if she had a plan

about what she would do when she got to Him. The ointment is expensive, even extravagant. It would have cost her much. In her line of business, we can only imagine that cost. It seems that what she had been given by Him when they met drove her to look for something to give Him in return. Precious for precious, perhaps knowing it wouldn't be enough. She *had* to worship Him. She *had* to do something to honor Him. She takes us with her into this unfolding holy drama. We scarcely can think or breathe.

When she gets close, it seems she cannot hold back the torrent of gratitude and love. The urgency in her worship of Jesus is arresting, causing our hearts to quicken. We are suddenly swept up in the moment with her. We are there with her at His feet, the feet of Jesus. She was driven, compelled, wholly abandoned. She throws herself at His feet in sheer beauty and sacred vulnerability, as though she can't get low enough before Him. The worship she offers is so extravagant, so exquisitely intimate that it is nearly embarrassing to witness. The gift she brought is not what was in the jar. She brought herself. She offered herself in worship at His feet.

We are left asking, What could be her motive? We will soon enough find out. We are now witnessing a woman caught up in worship, oblivious to social customs, with invulnerability to the fear of being judged or put to shame. After all, perfect love casts out fear.

This beautiful scene is being played out in the house of religious spirits, in a religious system inhospitable to those who do not measure up to the conventional standards. Because the woman of the city was a sinner, her offering is misjudged, mischaracterized, and misunderstood.

Perhaps it is because she has long been invisible in her community, or maybe it was because of her line of business, but she has

trained herself to ignore cultural and religious propriety. Still, her actions are very offensive when looked upon from the outside. The whole drama was awkward, embarrassing, undignified, and very politically and religiously incorrect. She is, indeed, a test. But not of Jesus' authority. It is a test of Simon's faith—and of ours.

From the outside looking in and seeing those reclining at the table, this prostitute rushes into the room and throws herself at the feet of this Man whom the people say is a holy man, even a prophet of God. She is weeping, and her tears wet His feet. Suddenly, without forethought, she loosens her hair to dry her tears from His feet, replacing them with kisses. Surely this prostitute knows that loose hair in public is a sign of a loose, immoral woman. A sinful woman.

Can you grasp this excruciating moment? Her beautiful act of worship appears to be a sensual manipulation from a known "sinner" in the city. To those who only saw the prostitute, her actions were shocking and disgusting. The loosening of her hair to wipe her tears from a man's feet only confirmed her status and affirmed the judgment heaped upon her. Now her seduction was exposed for all to see. She was *hamartia*—a condemned sinner. They judged that she, *and* Jesus, should be ashamed. Her worship defied the religious spirit and drew a line in the sand, exposing the system for what it was—blind and worshipless, unseeing and unsinging.

"Simon, Do You See?"

Now when the Pharisee who had invited him saw this, he said to himself, "If this man were a prophet, he would have known who and what sort of woman this is who is touching him, for she is a sinner."[18]

Before Jesus accepted the invitation to dinner, He had been with the crowds in the presence of several religious leaders. He had asked them what they went out to see when they went to see John the Baptist in the wilderness. He knew the answer, but He was leading them to look further and see something more. The sinners and tax collectors had gone out to see a prophet. John, indeed, was a prophet—and more. He was the prophet prophesied to be the forerunner to the Messiah, whose baptism stirred and exposed the religious system as corrupt and opposed to the purposes of God.[19]

The dinner guests had all witnessed the scandalizing scene between Jesus and the woman. The woman they already knew and had long ago judged. It was Jesus who was now being tried for judgment. Simon saw what was transpiring and formed his judgment in his mind. Now he knew, he thought. Jesus was no holy man, no prophet of God, for He allowed this brazen, seductive sinner to touch Him. Her touch physically transferred her spiritual and physical uncleanness to Him, and He permitted it. If He were a prophet, He would have—should have—rebuked and then shunned her. At once, when Simon had formed his professional religious opinion, one that Job's friends at least at one point in their lives would've applauded, Jesus said, "Simon, I have something to say to you."

He offers Simon a simple story with a message. "A certain moneylender had two debtors. One owed five hundred denarii, and the other fifty. When they could not pay, he cancelled the debt of both. Now, which of them will love him more?"[20] Simon answered, "The one with the big debt." It was the correct answer. Jesus leads him to focus on judging rightly, knowing Simon had judged Himself and the woman wrongly. He had no ability to see beyond them. Simon was blind. The religious spirit—the religious system he was bound by—blinded him.

Though a spiritual leader of the people who was known for the strictness of purity and holiness down to the smallest letter of the Law, he and others like him had "neglected the weightier matters of the law: justice and mercy and faithfulness," making them blind and unfit to lead people out of slavery into the promised goodness of God.[21]

Jesus is showing Simon, in His mercy and kindness, that he does not *see* beyond his judgments. "Simon, do you see this woman?" Jesus asks. Jesus knows Simon only sees a sinner acting sinfully. He does not *see* the woman. He does not *see* Jesus. The evidence is in Simon's lack of hospitality to both Jesus and the woman. Now Jesus is going to help Simon open his eyes to the something more before him.

> "Do you see this woman? I entered your house; you gave me no water for my feet, but she has wet my feet with her tears and wiped them with her hair. You gave me no kiss, but from the time I came in she has not ceased to kiss my feet. You did not anoint my head with oil, but she has anointed my feet with ointment. Therefore I tell you, her sins, which are many, are forgiven—for she loved much. But he who is forgiven little, loves little." And he said to her, "Your sins are forgiven."[22]

Forgiveness. This is the reason she worshiped. Unlike Simon, she knew she was a sinner. When her many sins were forgiven, her love, fueled by gratitude, overwhelmed any consideration of social or religious convention. She was a sinner saved by the grace of God. Her shame was gone, and though once a prostitute, she gave herself to Jesus in a physical expression of love and gratitude that, though misinterpreted by those around her, was innocent of sensual seduction, cleansed from the manipulation, exploitation, and abuse of her body by herself and others. She was free.

The Pharisee was not willing to do what the prostitute was desperate to do—prove her love. He did not see a need to. He had nothing to be grateful to Jesus for. He had invited Jesus to his house to test Him, not to serve Him. Simon served the system. Or more to the point, the system used Simon.

We can become so blind when we think we are serving God by following the predetermined conventions of a system created by religious spirits and blind guides. Religious spirits tell us our religious works are a testimony to our righteousness. Simon was blind to his own need for Jesus. He loved little, not seeing the enormous debt that he owed. Jesus—the Messiah—was in his house, but he did not bow in worship; his soul did not sing.

His religious spirit had deceived him into thinking he was superior. United with self-righteousness, he judged the woman a sinner and Jesus as a fraud, and he could not see his way to consider and judge his own sin. Even still, Jesus had come to sit at his table and hold out an opportunity for something more; healing for his blindness. Simon was blind to his need for a savior—for the Savior right in front of him. He did not know he was in the very presence of God.

The Worship That Defies a Religious Spirit

Then those who were at table with him began to say among themselves, "Who is this, who even forgives sins?"[23]

And with this question, from those at the table in the house of religious spirits, we find ourselves back at the beginning, full circle. Our story is about an unnamed woman (why, we should ask, does the Spirit keep her name from us?), caught in conflict with a religious system created by those who suppose themselves

superior, having worked to gain their status. They will not invite her to the table, welcoming her to sacred fellowship, but they may invite themselves to her bed to welcome and take advantage of her abasement. Why care? *She is only a woman. She is only a sinner.* Did you hear those words? That is the voice of the religious spirit that forever marginalizes, ostracizes, judges, and condemns, a voice that is void of mercy, compassion, and hospitality for God's creatures who are deceived and ravaged by sin and circumstance.

Who can hear a message of hope through a voice such as this? Abraham Heschel, a rabbinic scholar, explains:

> When faith is completely replaced by creed, worship by discipline, love by habit; when the crisis of today is ignored because of the splendor of the past; when faith becomes an heirloom rather than a living fountain; *when religion speaks only in the name of authority rather than with the voice of compassion, its message becomes meaningless.*[24]

The woman had been bound by her many sins, but she had also been bound by a religious spirit that shrouded her in shame, reminding her that she was unholy, impure, *and* without remedy. Then she meets Jesus—the God of justice, mercy, and compassion—who comes to make her clean, whole, and brand new. The Pharisees never did that. Rescued from her brokenness and the broken religious system, she offers up worship—free, whole, and brand new—that defies the religious spirit. It defies the religious spirit because she no longer wears her shame. She refuses to skulk around in the dark for fear of being called out for her sin or called upon for sexual favors. It is not who she is, even when she lets down her hair in public. And like Samson when his hair had grown back, she brings down the house.

In the end, her courage—her muchness—stirs everyone in the house to question what they thought they were seeing. They ask the most critical question in all of eternity: "Who is this, who even forgives sins?"[25] How many were there that day who were also bound by a system that forbade their welcome into the Kingdom? How many, like the woman, had lived under the designation, categorization, and reputation that kept them from being invited to the table to be healed and restored? Oh yes, there is a worship that defies a religious spirit.

Beholding in the Mirror

It's our turn. The woman who was a sinner asks you and me, "Do you see? Do you sing?"

Do you and I see that we are this woman? According to Scripture, we all have sinned and are undeserving of salvation. According to statistics, many women have, at one time or another, been victims of abuse, physical and sexual. One out of every three women globally has experienced abuse. I am one. Maybe you are, too. The strange thing about being the victim of abuse is that even when the abuse by the perpetrator ends, we may turn and continue to reenact the abuse by harming ourselves or engaging in dangerous behavior with others.[26] Whether living in sin or as the victim of sin, shame becomes an unwanted, persistent companion.

Adding to this dilemma, the religious spirit in the Church has placed boundaries and limitations on the identity and call on women's lives. Sometimes even downgrading our value, citing Eve's sin, so that if ever we let down our hair, we are immediately rejected and misjudged. In some regards, a stigma or veiled sense of shame is still attached to being female.

No one is safe from being judged when in the presence of a religious spirit, not male or female, young or old, rich or poor. Although it comes in many shapes and sizes, this system is always inhospitable to what it judges to be "the sinner," the victims of sin reenacting their abuse, sometimes (perhaps oftentimes) women called by God, and further, any who do not measure up to the erroneous measurements by which judgments are made.

In our story, as in so many other stories in the Bible, the woman shows us the way forward. She asks us to see beyond her forgiveness to the courageous worship that rejects rejection, breaks through the barriers, and reopens the doors of divine purpose. It reminds us of another marginalized, ostracized, unnamed woman at a well.[27] Meeting Jesus freed her from a life hidden and misjudged and sent her out in the fullness of the call on her life.

Do you see? Like the woman in our story and the woman at the well, our story doesn't end with seeing who Jesus is and the truth of all He has done—saved, healed, restored, cut off from past regret, and cleansed from shame and humiliation. It continues with singing—with worship. The loudest song you can ever sing is to walk in your calling without shame or apology, regardless of who is watching or judging. For you see, fulfilling the call on your life in the freedom that Jesus has given by the power of the Holy Spirit is the most courageous and extravagant worship you can give to Jesus. It will be the very thing that most deliberately and effectively defies the religious spirits of our day.

Does that make you sing?

8

Permission to Be *Me'od*— For the Sake of the World

OUR STORY

So the woman left her water jar and went away into town and said to the people, "Come."[1]

"Go into all the world and preach the gospel to all creation."[2]

*E*ACH CHAPTER IN THIS BOOK has challenged me to look deeper and further into the Bible to hear with fresh ears the stories of women heralded by the voice of the Spirit, who says "yes" and "amen" to their faithfulness, cunning, and courage, sanctioning their divinely directed mission in His world. Without a doubt, the Word of God gives full-throated-voice permission to each of us to be and do what He created us to be and to do in our *me'od—muchness*—for the sake of the world. I believe this. I believe it for me and for you.

What makes this chapter challenging to write has nothing to do with my beliefs. I have settled in my heart and mind, biblically and theologically, what I believe about women and their role in advancing the Kingdom of God. Still, I find myself wrestling with adding my small voice to a subject that is either widely held but too often left without application, or hotly contested. Ironic, considering this entire book is about *Finding Our Muchness*!

This chapter is about the theology of women coming into the fullness of their calling. From the moment I decided to write this book, I knew I wanted to include a chapter on this subject, feeling that it was important not only *for* you but *to* me to include it. It is important to me because at so many points in walking out the call on my life with Jesus, I have been confronted with sincere and sinister questions regarding my audacity to do so. There have been serious confrontations and denials related solely to my gender. While I have never felt the need to defend myself, debate, plead, or apologize, having a clear understanding that my permission comes from God and is grounded in Scripture is what keeps me. God's Word will keep you, too, as you navigate the world as a woman called by God.

Whether called to ministry, homemaking, nursing, business, teaching, or politics, this chapter is meant to help solidify for each of us that we have our Father's permission to be *me'od*—strong, courageous, intelligent, savvy, bold, and confident to rise into the fullness of the call on our lives. I have determined that I, too, will find my *me'od* and not shrink back from telling this story. The story in this chapter is ours—yours and mine.

Redefining Moments

I read somewhere that most people will experience one or two paradigmatic shifts in their lifetime in which nearly everything changes. One might experience a third, but it is rare. These shifts are what I call defining moments. They are moments when through God's providential working in our lives, circumstances align (or rather collide), making our hearts vulnerable to a lightning bolt of new truth that illuminates and transfigures our imprisoned and veiled perceptions of ourselves and the light we are meant to be to the world. Our identity and call—who we thought we were and what we were supposed to be about—are redefined in a flash.

Scripture is full of stories of transforming, transfiguring, divinely appointed, defining moments. Sometimes it happened before a burning bush, sometimes in an angelic encounter, and sometimes in changing a name. Still, it was always by God's grace. He loved His people too much to leave them or their futures defined by falsehoods, failings, and fortuity.

Psychologist and therapist Mel Schwartz writes about the importance of defining moments:

> Without insights we're shackled to a fixed and stagnating reality in which little changes. . . . Insights are the forerunners of our growth and personal evolution. . . . If you can't identify defining moments in your life, you've likely lived by the rules of conformity and have been influenced by fear.[3]

The Well-Woman

Scripture tells us that a specific woman seemed to be living by the rules of conformity and was influenced by fear.[4] Perhaps shame, rejection, or abuse were the conforming factors. Whatever the truth, she appears without name, anonymous and incognito in her own story, to draw water from a well in disconnection from her community. She'd had five husbands and the man she was living with was not her husband. Is she immoral? Is she unlucky? Is she cursed? Has she been abused, abandoned, divorced, or widowed these many times? We don't know. Scripture is silent on those details—perhaps precisely to draw out of us our preconceptions and biases.

If we rush to judge her based on the extrabiblical interpretations that have become conventional for us, we expose the hardness of our hearts and the slowness of our discernment. Based on what the text actually says, we know that she was living a fixed and stagnant reality, and Jesus was about to transfigure that reality so that she could find her muchness and rise to the fullness of her calling. She was to be instrumental in leading an entire city to faith. Having left her pot at the well, she herself becomes a vessel filled with living water and overflowing with the Spirit.

Everything—the time, place, and circumstances—seemed to hem her into her fixed reality. Conformity may not have been by her choosing. Too often, a version of a person's story becomes a fixed reality when assumptions are made and passed around to others. The assumptions become false imprisonment. Assumptions have been made about this woman who shows up at the wrong time in a place that is considered wrong (Samaria) by religious folk in her day who think they are in the right place at the right time. I love that Scripture tells us Jesus "had to go through Samaria"[5] to meet her because when God shows up at a well in Samaria at noon to speak to this woman, she is in the right place at the right time.

Even still, she was all wrong for everyone but Jesus. She was a Samaritan. She had a shadowy, sketchy past and present with six men. We don't know the reasons for her marriages or her current arrangement. And she was, well, a *she*—a woman. Each of these contexts required a certain cultural conformity, and each conditioned the living of a marginalized life. She did not possess the membership card—the right ethnicity, religious affiliation, gender, or social status—to enjoy favor and freedom in her community. She was an outcast, seemingly without the ability or opportunity to rise out of the caste appointed to her by the culture in which she lived. Survival depended on the water drawn by her hands from the well and the worth and status she could wring from belonging to a man.

She believed it. Her town believed it for her. Even the disciples believed it because they were shocked and tempted to be offended when they found Jesus talking to the woman. In a beautiful turning of the tables, the Holy Spirit in John's gospel uses that moment of shock and temptation to tell us that the all-wrong woman runs off to do the things the all-right disciples do not yet comprehend, much less do. As she is unreservedly entering into the mission of Jesus, gathering in the ripe harvest, the disciples marvel at the impropriety of their Master speaking to a woman.[6] As happens continually in the gospels, the insiders are the last to see the truth about Jesus, while the outsiders, especially the women and children, recognize Him and run to Him for help.

Yet, Jesus had come to the well just for her. He picked her. She was the first fruits of the fields ready for harvest. He knew she was ripe for a defining moment that would remove every label, limit, and lament that had conformed and imprisoned her in a reality not created by the One who had fearfully and wonderfully knit her together, embedding a gift and call waiting to be watered that could never be revoked, only rejected or suspended. He would transfigure it all into a story saturated with redemptive love to be told and retold to others dried up by the human experience. So Jesus met her to make her thirsty for what she longed for but had never tasted.

Three Demands

Masterfully, Jesus drew her in by three demands (expressed by the imperative verb form in Greek). Each is designed to open her heart and redefine the rules to which she had been conformed. If she conforms to His demands, she will find freedom from all that has falsely defined, fixed, and stagnated her reality. On the other hand, if she becomes offended, she may not come to faith, trusting the One who defines her as His own with the muchness that has always been His gift to and in her.

First, He said, "*Give* me a drink."[7] To serve Him, she would have to step across the label of uncleanness imposed by those she had been taught to consider and the boundaries of propriety set for her as a woman by her culture. As a Samaritan woman, she was considered by Jews to be unclean. What He is demanding of her is astounding! We know Jesus knew what He was asking of her when He asked it. We know Jesus is going about healing, casting out demons, bringing Good News, and scandalizing every false expectation of Himself, ourselves, and His Kingdom. In this way, we know that what He demands is not for His benefit but for hers in all those ways. Will she accept His demand on her life and step over the cultural lines drawn in the sand, or will she continue to live in conformity and fear?

She engages and moves closer. Jesus explains He is greater than her forefathers, and His gift is greater. Then the second demand comes, "*Call* your husband."[8] When I slow enough to feel these written words spoken to a woman who has had five husbands, living with a man who is not her husband, whose story has been told countless times with false assumption in her day and ours, it wrenches my heart. I feel her shame-induced suffering.

I am the daughter of divorced and remarried parents who were discounted in the Church with a nuanced rejection slight enough to go unnoticed by the general public but never unnoticed by us, ever lashing our family to the heretic's stake with fire never quenched. I feel her pain. Maybe you do, too. Could the woman from the well face her pain in the naming of it, not to claim it as a prefigured future, but to forsake it for a transfigured past that will become a new beginning?

She answers without excuse or defense and moves another step past the line drawn in the sand. She listens as Jesus reveals Himself as a prophet, telling her all she ever did. Her perception is changing quickly now. Could this be the Messiah?

Lastly, Jesus says, "Woman, *believe* me."[9] Now we, and she, come to it—the redefining defining moment. He wants *her*, not a drink from her well. He wants her heart. How long had it been since she was wanted for reasons pure and undefiled?

In a patriarchal culture, having a husband and children gave worth and status. She has had five husbands, and the covenant never lasted. Was her current relationship one of convenience? One of survival? Considering the five before, it is doubtful that it was one of love and promise. How could it have been since there was no covenant of marriage? It is not coincidental that Jesus met the woman at a well—the place of gathering, fellowship, community, and most important, betrothal. Jesus, the true patriarch, was seeking His bride.

Could she believe it? Could she bow her heart in worship, accepting this Man to be greater than the Law, the patriarchs, and all the lines that had been drawn negating that such a One would ever accept—no—*want* someone like her as His own? He had already told her things about her life He could not have known. Yet, in the flickering of faith, she dares to ask.

> The woman said to him, "I know that Messiah is coming (he who is called Christ). When he comes, he will tell us all things." Jesus said to her, "I who speak to you am he."[10]

The Divine Name! It's Him! And no sooner has He said it than her water jar is left behind, signaling the transfiguring of identity and call, transforming her past, present, and future. The line is not only crossed but erased in the sweeping silence of her having left the place where she once stood—fixed and stagnant—to fulfill the call on her life.

My Defining Moment

It is hard to describe how I felt when I heard, for my own ears, what so many like me have heard as they dare answer the call of God on their lives. When I say like me, I mean female. It was confusing, defeating, demoralizing, and very hurtful. All the questions I thought had been resolved surfaced with a vengeance, taunting me as I realized I could not articulate a defense for what I, a woman, was actively pursuing and already engaged in.

It was a beautiful sunny California morning in 2002. I was a jumble of emotion ranging from thrill to terror on the way to my first day of seminary. I started to fidget with the radio, looking for a worship station, sure that singing would help focus my mind and settle my stomach. The radio began scanning stations, stopping at each long enough for me to decide to make the selection or pass on. Suddenly, the voice of a well-known, celebrated, and influential preacher shot down my excitement midair. "The so-called doctrine of women in ministry is a doctrine of demons in the church," I remember him saying.

Just as suddenly, the hard-won confidence I'd nurtured, not about an illustrious career but that God had called me to the self-sacrificing work of preaching the Gospel to all the world, tore away at my edges, releasing a wail that rose in my chest and rushed out of my mouth. I was inconsolable. I hardly remember pulling into the school parking lot or making my way into the seminary advisor's office, but there I stood with tear-stained face, more than a little emotional.

Had I only imagined that God could call me to preach? Was it my pride and ambition calling me to leadership? Had I raised myself against Scripture? As a girl in the religious context in which I'd been raised, I knew I could sing in the choir, teach the women and children, and bring food to the potluck, but I had never seen a woman in the pulpit.

Oh God, I thought. *What am I doing? Can I even do what I came here to do?* After all, a woman does not go to seminary except to be trained for full-time vocational ministry, and she has no right to be in full-time vocational ministry if it's not scripturally supported. If the Word of God does not support a woman in ministry—a woman in ministerial/ecclesial leadership—then God has not spoken.

God *Has* Spoken

From the beginning of this book, the Holy Spirit, in story after story, has highlighted the participation of women in the mission of God with full permission from Him to walk in His call upon their lives, whatever and wherever it is, courageously, cunningly, and tenaciously. This is the point. It is the point Scripture makes and the point I hope this book is making. You have permission to be *me'od*—to find your *muchness*.

For several years now, I have sensed that the Holy Spirit was about to move unprecedentedly among women. It wouldn't be the first time such a thing has manifested when a revival movement of the Holy Spirit breaks out, as we historically understand it. Women will be raised up in every sector of society and ministry all over the world. I believe God desires to call back to the community of faith those women who were outcast by the Church, being encouraged or forced to use their gifts and talents elsewhere.

Many of the women I know long to serve the community of faith they belong to in meaningful and significant ways. They love their church but feel their gifts are not valued or welcomed. They are lawyers, doctors, financial consultants, TV producers, teachers, and administrators. They are homemakers, business leaders, and psychologists.

During my years as a senior executive pastor in the local church who was given a platform to preach and the authority to lead, oversee, and develop other leaders, and who was given the opportunity to execute vision within the ministry, strong women leaders from many sectors in the culture began attending our church. My presence and service were a sign of hope that women were welcome to bring themselves and their gifts to the table in service to Jesus.

Serving Jesus is a vital component of our Christian life. Roberta Hestenes reminds us, "It is impossible to grow in the Christian life if you are not involved in Christian service. Ministry is essential for Christian growth. It is a response to the love of God, and gives meaning and dignity to life."[11] I don't know about you, but even as a grandmother of six, I am not yet fully grown in Christ. I love to quote Tom Brady, former New England Patriots and Tampa Bay Buccaneers quarterback: "I didn't come this far to only come this far, so we've still got further to go!"[12]

For us to grow into the fullness of Christ, as it was with the well-woman, Photini (as she is named in the Christian tradition), Jesus may need to meet us in a defining moment that will beckon us to cross beyond cultural, religious, and gender lines drawn in the sand, breaking us free from a fixed and stagnant life lived by the rules of conformity and influenced by fear. Even in our day, when almost anything goes, many still question the calling and commissioning of women into the service of Christ. It isn't only men who label and limit women in the Church. It's women, too. All laboring under the influence of the principalities and powers that are arrayed against Jesus and His Kingdom.

Biblically Speaking

From chapter 1, the stories of women from Scripture have highlighted the divine blessing and support given to women who courageously served God in the face of danger, limitations, and misunderstanding. At this juncture, however, I want to examine Scripture without focusing on a story surrounding a specific female character. Instead, let's turn to what Scripture says about women as it pertains to women in ministry or leadership ministry. (This is a huge subject, and there are whole books on this topic and these passages. One chapter here will not cover every issue; therefore, I will summarize and give overviews and brief explanations. In the end, I will recommend several resources to assist with your research.)

Beginning with the book of beginnings, which sets precedent and is foundational for understanding what the Scripture teaches about men and women, Genesis tells us:

> Then God said, "Let us make man in our image, after our like-
> ness". . . . So God created man in his own image, in the image of
> God he created him; male and female he created them. And God
> blessed them. And God said to them, "Be fruitful and multiply
> and fill the earth and subdue it, and have dominion over the fish
> of the sea and over the birds of the heavens and over every living
> thing that moves on the earth."[13]

The Hebrew that is translated *man* in this passage means mankind, or humankind. All of humanity is created in God's image with worth and value. The image of God is present in men and women alike, equally and without distinction or hierarchy. This should be obvious to us, but historically it has not been, and we must not take it for granted that it always will be. The powers of this world are always working to destroy what God has made and to frustrate God's purposes. So, we must contend for the truth by rightly dividing Scripture and reasoning faithfully from what the Spirit shows us to be good and true.

It doesn't end there. Notice that the blessing and calling He gives is also given equally and without distinction or hierarchy to both the man and the woman. He tells them to be fruitful, multiply, and have dominion over all He has created. In other words, God is calling and commissioning the man and the woman to rule conjointly. They are to keep the divine order and to watch over and care for all God created the way God would. There is no distinction or hierarchy in authority mentioned in the passage.

This is the way it was supposed to be. Sin changed things. But first, let's discuss a woman's design.

The Matchmaker Makes a Match

"Then the LORD God said, 'It is not good that the man should be alone; I will make a helper fit for him.'"[14]

There has been much confusion over what this means. First, men and women were created by God to need one another. It is not good for any of us to be alone and without the help of another. There is no sense of hierarchy in this verse, but rather a sense of wholeness when we are together.

Second, and excitingly, in the original language, the words "helper fit for" are the words *ezer kenegdo*. The word *ezer* is found 21 times in the New Testament and is rendered overwhelmingly as "rescue/strength" or "strength/power." Sixteen times, it refers to God Himself and the help He brings. As Deuteronomy explains:

There is none like God . . . who rides through the heavens to your help, through the skies in his majesty. . . . And he thrust out the enemy before you and said, "Destroy." So Israel lived in safety. . . . Happy are you, O Israel! Who is like you, a people saved by the LORD, the shield of your help.[15]

The Hebrew word *kenegdo* should be rendered "equal and corresponding to."[16] When you put the two together, we can understand that God made woman to be a power/strength equal to and corresponding to man.

As my former seminary professor Dr. Wes Pinkham explains, "It is a tragic mistake to see Eve's creation as inferior to

Adam, as a mere helpmate." He points out that scholar Walter Kaiser resolved that the customary English translation of the two words as "helper fitting him" is undoubtedly wrong. Women were not created as inferior. Adam on his own was incomplete and deficient. God made for him a woman fully his equal and fully his match. "God created two powers who became complete, one. Both created strong and equal powers. Both created in the Image of God."[17] This is not to say that a woman is the same as a man. She is different and distinct, but equal.

In the beginning, the woman was created to receive and fulfill the covenantal blessing of fruitfulness and the divine call to have dominion over creation in full and complete partnership with the man. This is the way it was supposed to be, but sin marred and twisted it in a way it was not supposed to be.

Cursed and Distorted

The Fall into sin in the Garden fractured the relational dynamic between the man and the woman. The serpent was cursed for his part in the deception, and the ground was cursed because of the man.[18] For the woman, it is here that pain enters the relationship as the mutuality of their partnership is damaged and distorted. Before the Fall, the woman is not subordinated to the man; subordination is the fallout of the Fall into sin. What once was so good, although not yet perfected, is now not so good. From that time, women have desired to return to Edenic relational dynamics, struggling to climb out from under the effects of the curse. Jesus came to reverse the curse—and to bring about the fulfillment of that which Adam and Eve knew only by promise.

Moving Forward

As we have seen in the story of the woman at the well and the woman who was the sinner of the city in chapter 7, Jesus lifts women out of the limitations, labels, and labors placed on them unjustly. Even a casual reading of the gospels—Luke's gospel in particular—will bring to notice how Jesus elevates and promotes women. (I use the present tense because what Jesus says and does is never in the past only, but is also present and future.) He heals their diseases, welcomes them as disciples, receives their ministry to Him personally, and praises them for sitting at His feet and placing themselves under His tutelage.

The last mention above is a reference to the story of Martha and Mary.[19] For first-century, Middle East customs, sitting at the feet of a rabbi meant taking the position of a student to learn and be equipped. This was not a woman's place, according to the religious customs. Martha is upset not just because of the work that she is left to do but also because of Mary's audacity to break free from the traditional cultural definitions of what is possible for women in her day. And Jesus defends her.

N. T. Wright points out an essential consequence of Mary's audacity:

> Like much in the gospels, this story is left cryptic as far as we at least are concerned, but I doubt if any first-century reader would have missed the point. Examples like Mary's, no doubt, are at least part of the reason why we find so many women in positions of leadership, initiative, and responsibility in the early church.[20]

The twelve disciples were male for cultural reasons,[21] yet Jesus vitally included women in His life and ministry counter to the culture. He acted within and without cultural norms, maximizing

His ministry's effect for all people regardless of racial, socio-economic, or gender status.

Women are at the foot of the cross as He is crucified, women are the first at the tomb after His death, and women are the first to see and tell of His resurrection. This is a picture of discipleship. In fact, again to quote Wright, "This is of incalculable significance. If an apostle is defined as a witness to the resurrection, there were women who deserved that title before any of the men. Mary Magdalene and the others are the apostles to the apostles."[22]

Clothed with Power

Women are also found waiting and praying with the apostles in the Upper Room on the Day of Pentecost. They were all, without distinction or restriction, to be clothed with power when the promised Holy Spirit would be poured out upon them.[23] Imagine it. None fully understood what it all meant or what it would look like or how it would come. The anticipation must have been excruciating, ever-increasing with each passing minute.

Suddenly—a sound! The wind rushed in, and fire appeared upon their heads. They all were filled with the Spirit and began to speak in an unknown tongue. Together in one place, women and men experienced the pouring out of the promised Holy Spirit, clothing them with power from "on high," fulfilling the prophecies of Joel, Isaiah, Ezekiel, and Jeremiah.[24]

Just as Joel prophesied, the Spirit was poured out on all flesh, both male and female. All gave prophetic utterances declaring the wonders and majesty of God. All. No exclusion, no exception.

Peter then stands to prophesy the interpretation of the phenomena—the Holy Spirit has been poured out on all flesh, and it is for all people, every generation regardless of gender, race, age, or socioeconomic status, eternally.[25] The clothing with power is for everyone. In fact, according to the author of Hebrews, the Holy Spirit and His gifts are poured out and distributed according to God's will without discrimination as to gender or color.[26]

Sadly, and importantly, as Pentecostal scholar and professor Estrelda Alexander points out, "Arguments against the ministries of women are seldom confined to criticisms of women in ministry. They are usually attacks on the prophetic, Spirit-empowered view of ministry that the Pentecostal movement inherited from [Phoebe] Palmer."[27] Spirit-empowerment is given for effective proclamation of the Gospel for the sake of the world. Ministry is not gender-based; it is gift-graced. There are good differences that God has established between men and women, and differences nature and the conventions of our cultures have established, for good and for bad. But none of these differences limit the flow of the Spirit that "bloweth where it listeth."[28]

The rest of Acts and the New Testament is filled with the stories of men and women doing just that. Women serve and lead as founders of churches,[29] teachers, pastors, prophets, evangelists, and apostles.[30] Peter describes all followers of Christ as chosen and part of the holy, royal priesthood.[31] According to John, Jesus made us all to be a Kingdom as priests to serve God and reign over the earth with Christ.[32] Indeed. This is who we are as part of the whole Body of Christ.

So, What about Paul?

According to Paul, men and women are without distinction in value, status, or authority in Christ.[33] When we look at Paul's writings in 1 Corinthians, we find instructions for the whole Church (not just men) in the proper practice of the gifts of the Spirit, especially in prophecy and in loving, faithful conduct and character.[34] Scholar and Anglican priest Kevin Giles writes:

> Paul's teaching on the ministry of the body of Christ presupposes that the Spirit bestows the same gifts of ministry on men and women. When it is recognized that Paul's theology of ministry is predicated on nondiscriminatory Spirit empowerment, we are then able to properly understand the three texts where he regulates harmful behavior in the church involving women—1 Corinthians 11:3–16, 14:33–34, and 1 Timothy 2:11–12.[35]

The three texts Giles is referring to are the three texts that are commonly misunderstood and placed as prohibitions on ministry for women. This short section will be more pragmatic and less narrative than the others for reasons I trust will be evident.

Let's begin with 1 Corinthians in the order they appear below:

> The women should keep silent in the churches. For they are not permitted to speak, but should be in submission, as the Law also says. If there is anything they desire to learn, let them ask their husbands at home. For it is shameful for a woman to speak in church.
>
> 1 Corinthians 14:34–35

> But I want you to understand that the head of every man is Christ, the head of a wife is her husband, and the head of Christ is God. Every man who prays or prophesies with his head covered dishonors his head, but every wife who prays or prophesies with her head uncovered dishonors her head, since it is the same as if her head were shaven. For if a wife will not cover her head, then she should cut her hair short. But since it is disgraceful for a wife to cut off her hair or shave her head, let her cover her head.
>
> 1 Corinthians 11:3–6

When Paul writes his instruction to limit speech, he is not referring to teaching, prophesying, or ministry, but rather in regard
to keeping orderly service in the church. We know this because
in 1 Corinthians 11:3–6, he speaks of women (specifically wives)
praying and prophesying in the church without covering their
heads, essentially instructing women how to dress and groom
themselves when engaging in public leading and speaking. Silence in the churches, then, cannot be a universal principle for all
women and for all time. Instead, it must be situational—specific
to a situation.

Now participating in the early Church, women coming out
of Judaism were far less likely to be educated than men. As they
were listening to Scripture being exegeted, they did not understand and had many questions that they were asking in the moment. The asking disrupted the service. Paul acknowledges their
desire and God-given permission to learn, which was radically
countercultural. Still, he instructs them to ask their questions at
home from male family members who could answer them. New
Testament scholar Craig Keener tells us Paul's point was not to
prohibit women from either learning or ministering in the service, but that "those who do not know the Bible very well should
not set the pace for learning in the Christian congregation."[36]

Paul's exhortation regarding head coverings refers to cultural
norms for men and women. Though they are equal in status,
value, and authority in Christ, they are differentiated in gender.
Although he also endorses their leadership and ministry, Paul
asks wives in the Corinthian church to acknowledge that their
behavior and dress can bring reproach to their family and the
church. As Keener points out, nothing in this passage suggests
a wife's subordination; appealing to the creation story affirms
that men and women are mutually dependent in the Lord. Since

women have authority over their heads, they ought to demonstrate it through modesty.[37]

Finally, we come to the firebomb in Timothy that consumes the *muchness* and burns to ash all hope of rising to the fullness of the call for so many women.

> Let a woman learn quietly with all submissiveness. I do not permit a woman to teach or to exercise authority over a man; rather, she is to remain quiet. For Adam was formed first, then Eve; and Adam was not deceived, but the woman was deceived and became a transgressor. Yet she will be saved through childbearing—if they continue in faith and love and holiness, with self-control.
>
> 1 Timothy 2:11–15

The first time you read those four words, "I do not permit," they feel so harsh. We have examined a large swath of Scripture. Can it be that Paul negates everything we have understood thus far with these four words and four sentences? Can it be that he negates his own teaching that he gave in other contexts? Can it be that he undercuts the goodness of the Good News for all women everywhere? No, he does not. Paul's concern in his letter to Timothy, who lives in Ephesus, is false teaching.

In a lengthy examination of the original languages and historical context, Keener concludes that women who are unlearned and ignorant of Scripture are to be silent and not take to themselves the authority to teach others.[38] No one should do such a thing, male or female, but Paul is addressing a specific situation in Ephesus. To handle the responsibility of teaching the Word of God, a woman must be educated. Why the mention of Adam and Eve? To this point N. T. Wright reminds us:

[Paul's] basic point is to insist that women, too, must be allowed to learn and study as Christians, and not be kept in unlettered, uneducated boredom and drudgery. Well, the story of Adam and Eve makes the point: look what happened when Eve was deceived. Women need to learn just as much as men do. Adam, after all, sinned quite deliberately; he knew what he was doing, he knew that it was wrong, and he deliberately went ahead.[39]

Unfortunately, the apostle Paul has been used to place limitations on women who desire to fulfill a call to ministry when neither his theology nor practice of ministry approves of such. Yet, as found in his other writings, Paul, like Jesus, praises and supports Christian women who prophesy, teach, preach, plant, and lead in the Church.[40] Scripture does not place limits on what women can be called to do.

Historically Speaking

Throughout history, brave Christian women have had an impact on and influenced society. They led movements and had an impact on generations even when the culture into which they were born limited women in ministry. Here is a quick historical overview of a few of my favorites.

In the 1400s, Joan of Arc in France was visited by the voice of God through angelic messengers. At sixteen years old, she dared to request to lead the nation's armies to restore the throne to the rightful king of France and free the nation from the grip of England. She succeeded in her quest.

In the 1500s, Saint Teresa of Ávila, a Carmelite nun and mystic, wrote the famous book *The Interior Castle*, which guided millions of people into the presence of God. Her book is still read today.

In the 1600s, Susanna Wesley was responsible for teaching and mentoring her two revivalist sons, John and Charles Wesley.

In the 1800s, Harriet Tubman formed the Philadelphia Female Anti-Slavery Society. She was a Christian who escaped slavery and went on to lead an influential movement within the Underground Railroad, personally saving hundreds of enslaved people.

Florence Nightingale, a social reformer and founder of modern-day nursing, fought to improve health care for wounded soldiers. Her efforts improved health care for all.

In the nineteenth century, Phoebe Palmer was a prominent leader in the Holiness movement. She played a significant role in spreading the concept of Christian holiness worldwide. Palmer defended the idea of women in Christian ministry in her book *The Promise of the Father*, which continues to influence the theology of women today.

Francis Willard, leader of the Temperance Movement with its two million members, led the way in protecting society from alcoholism, assisted in passing child labor laws, and started kindergartens and daycare for the children of working families.

In the twentieth century, the Missionary Movement was led by women. Eight hundred and fifty-six single women missionaries were sent into the world, and the campaign led to translating the Bible for hundreds of language groups.

Carrie Judd Montgomery and Maria Woodsworth-Etter were recognized worldwide as powerful and anointed leaders in the Healing Movement.

Aimee Semple McPherson, a healing evangelist and preacher, became the most recognized and prominent woman leader of the Pentecostal Movement. She founded the International Church of the Foursquare Gospel, now found in more than 150 countries with 6.7 million members and 64,377 churches.[41]

Historian Vinson Synan writes of Sister Aimee's impact:

> The advent of Aimee Semple McPherson marked a turning point in the history of Pentecostal movement. . . . The first Pentecostal well-known to the public at large. . . . Indeed "Sister Aimee" proved that Pentecostals were capable of producing preachers with as strong a public appeal as . . . Charles G. Finney and Dwight L. Moody.[42]

Who can forget Kathryn Kulhman? She was one of the most well-known healing evangelists in history. Yet, these are only a few examples of the women throughout history who dared to answer the call of God on their lives.

They believed in something greater than themselves. They believed that the Gospel could change the world. Their hearts burned with passion for the lost, the broken, the sick, the poor, the widow, and the orphan. They looked at society and the culture of their day and lifted their voices, offered their hands and feet, and laid down their lives to create something better, something holier, something pleasing to the heart of God. Listen to Florence Nightingale:

> If I could give information of my life, it would be to show how a woman of very ordinary ability has been led by God in strange and unaccustomed paths to do in his service what he has done in her. And if I could tell you all, you would see how God has done all, and I nothing. I have worked hard, very hard, that is all, and I have never refused God anything.[43]

I pray Jesus uses the words of this chapter to lead you into your own defining moment. Women change the world when they dare to break free and refuse to live by rules of conformity and be influenced by fear. We have permission to "never refuse God anything," and to be *me'od*—much, much more than we or anyone else in our world have imagined we could be. We belong to God and God's Kingdom, not the kingdoms of this world. He defines us and authorizes us to live our definition to the full.

For further study:

1. Kevin Giles, *What the Bible Actually Teaches on Women* (Eugene, OR: Cascade Books, 2018).
2. J. Lee Grady, *10 Lies the Church Tells Women: How the Bible Has Been Misused to Keep Women in Spiritual Bondage* (Lake Mary, FL: Charisma House, 2000).
3. Susan C. Hyatt, *In the Spirit We're Equal: The Spirit, the Bible, and Women, A Revival Perspective* (Dallas, TX: Hyatt Press, 1998).
4. Cindy Jacobs, *Women, Rise Up!: A Fierce Generation Taking Its Place in the World* (Bloomington, MN: Chosen Books, 2019).
5. Carolyn Moore, *When Women Lead: Embrace Your Authority, Move Beyond Barriers, and Find Joy in Leading Others* (Grand Rapids: Zondervan, 2022).

CONCLUSION

Alice laughed. "There's no use trying," she said: "one can't believe impossible things." "I daresay you haven't had much practice," said the Queen. "When I was your age, I always did it for half-an-hour a day. Why, sometimes I've believed as many as six impossible things before breakfast."[1]

The Lord gave the word; great was the company of those who proclaimed it.[2]

One Sunday at church, I preached a message created from a chapter in this book. At the end of the message, a memory flashed into my mind of an experience I'd had that had a profound impact on me. I was on mission in Brazil. I had just finished praying for the prayer and healing team members who had flown in from around the world to minister with me for the following eight days. Business leaders, nurses, pastors, psychologists, homemakers, and plumbers were among them. All were excited to be part of a mission trip, ready to lay hands on the sick, and eager to see them recover.

Orientation was now completed. Two pastors approached asking if they could pray for me. Absolutely! As they laid hands on me, I fell to the floor under the power of the Holy Spirit and entered a vision. At first, there was nothing but blank white space. I heard a voice, and I knew it was Jesus. How I knew, I don't know. I only know that I knew. He said, "Kimmy (my childhood nickname), someone here wants to see you."

I did not know what or who to expect, so I waited. In a moment of sheer surprise, my mom came before me. She kissed my cheek, took my face in her hands, and looked deeply into my eyes. Then, suddenly, she was gone, and the vision was over. I broke into soft weeping.

The last time I had seen my mother alive, she was dying of cancer. She had been sick for a long time. My sister, brother, and I cared for her and my father in the final weeks of her illness. I was alone with her in her last moments—in her last breath. She did not look like herself. She didn't look like my mom.

Yet, in the vision, she was more than recognizable, she was—herself. She was not skinny and sick. She was not looking at me with haunting, suffering eyes that belied her fear and begged for a rescue I could not give. She embodied all the memories I cherish about her from the days of my childhood through to the moment she was changed by her illness—smiling, giggling, white-haired, but not old. Her transfiguration transfigured my loss of her. She was very alive, very beautiful, and I knew she was very happy. Immediately, my disfigured memories of her were undone.

Something passed between us. I knew I had received a "mother's blessing" and mantle—permission to take my place as a leader, mother, and matriarch. It was a very personal touch of kindness from the Lord. This kind of blessing He could have arranged for me to receive from any number of women leaders I have relationships with. Still, it came from my own mother, healing and expanding my heart.

The experience instilled a sense of legacy in my heart. The story of her courage to raise three children on her own after moving away from family, her home state, and everything she had known—having been abandoned by her husband at the age of 23—lives on through me. There is a revival of all she achieved, dreamed, hoped, and prayed for herself and me.

I come from a long line of courageous women who braved the sufferings and challenges of life to give themselves and their children something more than they started with. They loved their families, and they loved Jesus. Each generation went further than the one before.

Now it was my turn. The Lord saw to it that I receive the blessing, approval, and permission of my mother for who I am and what I am doing with my life. I received her blessing to be free to take my place and go further, fly higher, and accomplish more in my generation than my mother had in hers. Having experienced the richness and freedom it has given me, I now know the importance of someday passing it on to my daughters. If I go two miles, perhaps they will go five; and if they go five, perhaps my granddaughters will go ten. And not my daughters and granddaughters only, but also my son and grandsons. They need blessing from me, too, without prohibition or restraint, to know they are loved, believed in, and have permission to live God's dream for them. I hope all my children will go further in their generation than I have in mine, accomplishing all God has planned for them.

When this experience flashed into my mind at the end of the service, I felt moved by the Lord to pray a mother's blessing over those present in the service, whether male or female. When I asked for those who felt the need for such a thing in their life to stand, I was overwhelmed with compassion. Nearly all in the room stood. I acknowledged their need, asking them to allow me to stand in for their mother, whether living or gone, as a mother in the Church. Tears flowed all over the room that morning.

Think with me for a moment. Nearly all stood. They stood and admitted, publicly, to having missed a mother's blessing, yet still feeling the need and desire to receive one—a blessing from the women who held the most authority in the most vulnerable years of their lives. This was a sign to me. It ought to be a sign to you as well. Do you remember when we spoke about the meaning of signs in chapter 5?

Signs convey information. They point, mark, remind, describe, welcome, and warn. They are messages that require not only our attention but also our interpretation to gain the insight contained in them. If we miss or misinterpret them, we fail to receive understanding needed to make decisions—sometimes critical decisions. Missing a sign can be fatal. Not only for us but also for others.

If nearly everyone inside a church has this felt and genuine need, what about outside the church? Women and the ministry they offer are not only needed; they are necessary. If mankind, being made male and female, are the image of God, how can the fullness of God on the earth be seen, represented, and experienced without women?

Each story contained in this book has been told in a way that highlights the gift women are and the vital life and ministry they carry. Each chapter describes the indelible impact women of faith have on circumstances, cities, families, and nations when they find their *me-od* and dare to act. The stories of these eight biblical women are not meant to be the *opus magnum* of the women in Scripture; they are only the overture. There are many more women and many more stories. Each woman is like a musical note, and each story is a movement, adding to God's masterfully composed and conducted symphony. The faithful offer melodies and harmonies, while the unfaithful rise in sharps and fall in flats. In any case, each is worth hearing and pondering in our hearts.

The women I chose to include in this book are those who, over the course of my life of following Jesus and answering a unique call to ministry, captured my imagination and inspired me to take risks to go further, reach higher, and sing my own song. In each chapter, I have wrestled with doubts about the sound of my own voice. I have asked myself, even chided, if I had any right to speak for these women and about these women to the women who may read this book.

I have used their stories to help create a world where we all may feel we are part of the worship rising to God and have permission from God, Scripture, and history to sing our songs. I suppose the ones left who need to give their permission are us. You to you, and you to each other. Permission has been granted so that we can wholeheartedly step into whatever the Lord is asking of us, and then turn to extend permission, support, and celebration to other women around us who are pursuing the call.

As I told their stories in every chapter, I would see a parade of faces. The parade begins with my grown daughters, daughter-in-law, and her sisters, extending to girlfriends and colleagues, women at my home church, and the many women I have met over years of ministry and in my travels. I also see my son's face and the faces of the young men to whom I am a spiritual mother, the husbands of the young women I mentor, and most important for my heart, the faces of my six beautiful grandsons.

This book is not written *for women only*. The stories I have told are scriptural stories. Each chapter and every story, like the Great

Commission in Matthew, is given to the whole Body of Christ, who, being male and female, are called "for such a time as this" for the sake of the world. Ultimately, this book is not about women or men, but the heart of God, who so loved the world that He gave His Son. Ultimately, this book is about reaching the world with the love of Christ. For that, we need women and men who are strong, courageous, and cunning. We need women and men to rise to the fullness of their calling.

Toward the end of the *Alice in Wonderland* movie, Alice is standing in full armor with her sword in hand looking radiant but terribly small before a goliath of a dragon, ferocious in appearance and reputation. The prophecy foretold that Alice was the champion who would slay the dragon, and at first glance, no one, not the Red Queen, the dragon, the moviegoers, nor Alice, can imagine this is possible.

We watch with anxious anticipation as she gathers her courage in spurts and sputters, gripping her sword ever tighter, until she calls to her remembrance a familiar anthem: "Sometimes, I believe in six impossible things before breakfast." To which her friend, the Mad Hatter, responds, "That is an excellent practice!" She steadily builds her courage by recounting the six impossible things she believes: "One. There's a potion that can make you shrink. Two. And a cake that can make you grow. Three. Animals can talk. Four, Alice. Cats can disappear. Five. There's a place called Wonderland. Six. *I can slay the Jabberwocky.*"[3]

The prophecy has been fulfilled. The Holy Spirit has been poured out, and His gifts have been distributed according to His will. He clothes you with power from on high to slay the dragon in your generation. You will need to find your muchness, and you can. I believe in you! Girlfriend, you have been empowered by the Holy Spirit to slay the devils and devilish systems of this world that loom large like giants of old, terrifying people—children, men, and women—threatening to kill, steal, and destroy. The devil is a liar. The battle is won. And God has a victory for you to announce and a Gospel for you to proclaim.

King David writes, "The Lord gave the word; great was the company of those who proclaimed it."[4] The great company doing the proclaiming is female. Miriam announced the victory of God over the earthly king who thought he was a god and his oppressive, systematic slavery at the Red Sea. In the Magnificat, Mary announced the victory of God over the proud powerbrokers and corrupted political systems that enslave the vulnerable.[5] Another Mary announced the victory of God, the Son, who defeated death and hell at the resurrection.

I prophesy over you today that there is a great company of bold, courageous, and cunning women—women who have found their *muchness*—rising in our day to sing, announce, and proclaim the Good News of Jesus. The call has gone out from the moment we were created, in the beginning. This is our heritage and inheritance. It's time to know who we are, hear the call on our lives, and discover the power within us. The world is waiting for us to start believing for impossible things.

My friends and sisters, *for the sake of the world, I pray you will find your muchness and rise into the fullness of the call!* When you do, I will cheer you on, celebrating all God accomplishes in and through your life.

Before We Go

I'd like to go back for a moment to the story about the vision of my mom I felt led to share on a Sunday morning. Just as I felt the nudge of the Spirit on that morning, I feel it now. Perhaps you, like me, never received a mother's blessing from your own mom. After reading my story, you long for one. Perhaps your mother was taken from you too early by sickness or tragedy. Perhaps she abandoned you out of her own dysfunction or sin-sickness. Maybe she simply did not understand the power of blessing and did not receive it herself. Whatever the reason, and there are many, I believe it is of such importance for us all right now.

May I entreat you to open your heart to the Spirit and give me your permission to pray for you and release a Mother's Blessing over you?

The Prayer

Father, in the name of Jesus, I ask You, as a mother to my own children and to Yours, to come in Your great mercy and compassion to heal all who read these words. Heal them of any wounds they carry from their mothers and/or women leaders from being overlooked, dismissed, discounted, invisible, neglected, abused, unloved, rejected, unprotected, and saddled with unrealistic expectations they could never meet. Father, wherever their needs, hearts, and requests as a child went unheard and unseen, heal those places. Wherever they still carry grief over a mother who left through divorce, abandonment, sickness, or tragedy, come near the brokenhearted as only You comfort, heal, and restore. Now, Father, I stand in the gap for the sins and shortcomings of these mothers and ask for Your forgiveness and for a release over these sons and daughters of the grace of the Spirit and the power of the blood of Jesus, enabling them to forgive. Please, Father, command any demonic spirit of grief, torment, and despair to be broken and removed. I command, in the name of Jesus, that the heavy burden of unforgiveness lift off them right now as they choose to forgive and receive freedom. I invite You, Holy Spirit, to come minister and fill them right now. In Jesus' name, Amen.

The Blessing

As the Lord made me a mother, in my family and in the Church, I stand in that role and bless you with a mother's blessing that comes from Him, through Him, and because of Him to bring you to Himself, make you whole and complete in His love. I bless the gift that you are—to your family and the world—given by God. You were carefully handcrafted by the Lord to fulfill a very special purpose that will touch the hearts and lives of those around you.

I bless your heart to be pure in passion and devotion. I bless your life to be abundant and experience the life, love, and faithfulness of Christ. I bless your unique personality and purpose as good because it was created by God before you were born. I bless you as a mother, giving you permission to do and be everything God dreams for you to be, to be free to go further and achieve more than I have without fear of failure, competition, jealousy, abandonment, or rejection because you do.

I give you permission to rise as high as the Lord will take you, and to walk in the fullness of the call on your life. I bless your potential, your passion, and your calling. I bless your *muchness*— the courage and cunning and tenacity that is in you. I bless your marriage, your children, and the work of your hands. I ask the Lord to bless your household and give you joy, peace, grace, favor, hope—and above all else, faith and love. *In the name of our Lord Jesus, I bless you. Amen.*

FINDING
OUR MUCHNESS
TEN-DAY DEVOTIONAL

It isn't over. Not by a long shot. It's not meant to be until the day
when all things are made new for eternity. The stories of these
women and the ground they took belong to you now, and their
stories are meant to live on, in and through you, as you step into
the story of Scripture, taking your place in the halls of faith. The
women you read about in this book are now a great heavenly
company, peering over the walls of eternity, cheering you on as
you follow in the way as part of the great earthly company of
women who announce the Good News, carrying forward the
Kingdom of our God. Someday, you and I will join them, cheering on the women who follow behind us generations from now.

Until then, I have created ten devotions from a few of the most
powerful truths in each story, adding applicational thoughts and
a brief prayer to help you on your way. As with the chapters, I
arranged them the way that seemed best to me as I placed my

heart and hands in the hands of the Spirit. Please feel free to do the same. Start at the beginning, the end, or anywhere in between. You can read them at the close of their corresponding chapters or keep them as a devotional series for when you have finished the entire book. It doesn't have to be one or the other, either. You may want to do both.

You can devote ten days only or commit to ten days times three for a month of *Muchness* devotions. Or start with these and write another ten, twenty, thirty, or fifty of your own. Even better, gather the women around you and start a *Muchness* club to read and pray through the book, sharing your thoughts and devotions and encouraging one another.

In any case, devotions do their most profound work when you can savor by reading slowly, journaling all along the way, and praying through the thoughts that come to mind—without distraction. So, I suggest setting aside a specific time and place to pray and listen. Have a Bible and a journal close at hand. Then, spend a few minutes in worship, inviting the Holy Spirit to lead, speak, and inspire you. Read through the devotion, meditate on the verses provided, and allow the Spirit of God to bring the fullness of His thoughts and intentions to your heart and mind. Write down your thoughts. Pray back to God what you hear, all in the name of Jesus, and then listen for more. If you do this, you will find that your muchness has been *in there*—on the inside of you, placed by Creator God's loving hand—all along.

It's your time. It's your turn. Rise into the fullness of your call!

You Are Powerful

> You shall love the LORD your God with all your heart and with
> all your soul and with all your *me'od*.
>
> Deuteronomy 6:5

> Therefore do not throw away your **confidence**, which has a great
> reward. For you have need of endurance, so that when you have
> done the will of God you may receive what is promised.
>
> Hebrews 10:35–36

You are powerful. You have the power, the creativity, the agency—
thanks to God!—to change your life, relationships, world, and
the world around you. You do not have to live with a broken
heart, broken relationships, or a broken world. Today, Jesus can
change your mind from the heart outward and fill you with the
power of the Holy Spirit to bring that same change to bear in the
lives of others anywhere and everywhere He sends you. You are
anointed, appointed, and called by God to have an impact on the
world in exactly the ways God needs you to. Scripture and history
bear witness to the truth that women, young and old, married
and single, known and unknown, favored and disfavored, are
powerful, and you have a vital, life-giving part to play in God's
plan for your life and the lives of others.

Today, resolve that you will find your *me'od—muchness—*and take back what is missing. With the confidence of who God says you are and what He has called you to do that got lost in the confusion, troubles, and uncertainties of life, take back the power, force, or essence. You were not born to find a comfortable place and stay there. You were born to be a champion, to push back the darkness, and to advance the Kingdom.

PRAYER

Father, in the name of Jesus, heal, restore, and change my heart and mind so that I know without a doubt that I am powerful. Fill me again with Your Holy Spirit, clothing me with power. I come out of agreement with any lie or any unspoken, unhealthy, and unholy rules, or any corrupt systems that have bound me with doubt, guilt, shame, and fear about who I am and what I am called to. Forgive me for throwing away my confidence in what You have spoken to me about who You are, who I am, and Your ability to bring to pass all You have spoken. I believe I am powerful because You made me so! In Jesus' name, Amen.

You Are Invited

> And God said to Abraham, "As for Sarai your wife, you shall not call her name Sarai, but Sarah shall be her name. I will bless her, and moreover, I will give you a son by her. I will bless her, and she shall become nations; kings of peoples shall come from her."
>
> Genesis 17:15–16

Sarah is not just a tagalong—someone who accompanies but is not invited to have any truly significant role in the plan. Instead, her name change is an invitation to partner with God and Abraham for the sake of the world. As the mother of nations, Sarah was called to stand beside Abraham, the father of nations.

You, too, are invited to partner with God for the sake of the world. He calls you by name and has a plan for you. Wherever the perceptions you have of yourself don't match God's perceptions, you are not yet standing in your true identity. You've not yet grown into the definitions set for you by the Spirit. Remember, God gives no blessing or favor *to a false identity*. There is only pressure to perform, pressure to meet every false expectation other people will have for us. You are God's beloved. He fashioned you in your mother's womb and set you in this time and place as the unique creation you are because He delights in you. His purpose in your generation depends on you. *All blessing, favor, and Holy Spirit empowerment come with our identity and call in Christ Jesus if we believe.*

God is calling you out to rise up and not live as though you are unworthy, without value and something to offer, no longer believing you are without authority and power to make a difference, no longer intimidated to remain silent in the face of injustice. God is calling you to *throw out the bondwoman*—the slavery, bondage, and false identities that keep you not hardly yourself.

PRAYER

Father, in the name of Jesus, I want every blessing and all the favor and power You desire to pour out on my life. I reject every perception of myself that You do not have of me. I reject the pressure to perform. Heal and deliver me from any false identity that keeps me not hardly who You say I am. I accept Your invitation to partner with You for the sake of the world. In Jesus' name, Amen.

DAY THREE:

You Are Not Done

And they came to Bethlehem at the beginning of barley harvest.

Ruth 1:22

With God, the end is only the beginning. Nothing is impossible for God. God makes all things new. Sometimes, however, you have to make room for that new vision. You have to stop investing your energy, time, or money on what has stopped producing fruit. You will have to resist the temptation to stay where things are familiar, and you must turn and go where there is fresh bread— where God is present and presently working.

It is a more complicated way to live than it sounds when I say it. I know. Sometimes, given the resistances you're forced to face, the doubts that assail you, the afflictions within and without, you become heartsick and give up hope. But remember that God is with you even—especially!—when it seems He isn't. This story reminds us of that deep truth. He moved on behalf of Ruth and Naomi behind the scenes after tragedy and crisis had taken almost everything in their lives.

Keep following the voice of God, and don't listen to the voice of reason. If you put your faith in what reason says, you won't hope for anything beyond what you see within arm's reach. Don't listen to bitterness, either. Bitterness narrows vision. It distorts

211

faith, rejects hope, disowns joy, and distrusts love. If you put your faith in what bitterness says, you will never trust anyone again—not even God. You might exchange the promises for the familiar, and your voice will be emptied of its authority. Lastly, don't trust the voice of conformity. It will make you fear failure and doubt your decision to *risk starting over.* If you take the risk, God will position you to receive a redemptive harvest for your life and the lives of others.

PRAYER

Father, I know that You are always working. You never stop working, even when I am not aware. There will be, and maybe there are now, places in my heart and circumstances in which I am living that feel dead. I reject carnal reason, bitterness, and conformity. Speak to me. Give me the faith to know that an ending can be a new beginning with You. Please call me forward, give me hope and strength to start over, and I will respond. In Jesus' name, Amen.

DAY FOUR:

You Have a Voice

"The daughters of Zelophehad are right. You shall give them possession of an inheritance among their father's brothers. . . . 'If a
man dies and has no son, then you shall transfer his inheritance
to his daughter. . . . And it shall be for the people of Israel a statute
and rule, as the LORD commanded Moses.'"

Numbers 27:7–11

You have a part to play in the unfolding history of God's Kingdom
on earth. Sometimes you will come up against things that are not
right. In the midst of that injustice, oppression, or bias, you will
need to take a stand and speak up.

The daughters of Zelophehad spoke without precedent or
guarantee of outcome, asking to be counted among the men and
receive an inheritance. They asked for a change in a law, requir-
ing an answer from God for reformation. It wasn't against the
rules, but *it wasn't in the rules*. It was not a question of provision,
but whether daughters—girls—were suitable heirs of the future
God had promised. They refused to settle for less. The day they
stepped forward to take a stand and speak up, they changed the
world and made history for generations of women.

You have a voice to raise over what breaks the heart of God.
You can call for change without calling down the judgment of
God on anyone. In raising your voice, you will be seizing the

opportunity to change the rules and gain the fullness of the inheritance God has for us and for the generations of women coming behind us. Refuse to settle for less. *Find your voice.* And give your heart so completely to Christ that He can speak in your voice and your words, bringing His words to life. That is the kind of prophetic action that will change the world.

PRAYER

Father, You have created me for this exact time to make history and pioneer the way for the generations coming behind me. Please help me find my voice. Give me the courage to speak boldly and the wisdom to speak righteously to the injustices of my day. In Jesus' name, Amen.

You Can Lead

"For the LORD will sell Sisera into the hand of a woman."

Judges 4:9

God hears the cries of the oppressed and suffering. He hears them as His own cry, the cry of His children, His Bride. He appoints women and men to be His partners and instruments of salvation and deliverance. Rahab's shrewdness helped fell Jericho, Esther's political savvy prevented a holocaust, the unnamed wise woman's clever negotiations ended a murderous rampage, much as Abigail did, and Deborah and Jael's daring leadership ended a tyrannical reign of terror.

Jael didn't kill Sisera because he was a man. We do not wrestle against flesh and blood, but against devils and dark powers. She killed him because he was evil, and when evil came near her tent, she drove a tent peg through its head! She didn't wait until her husband came home. She didn't compromise, beg, or politely ask it to leave. She didn't wait to hear what it had to say. She did not open herself or her household to it. She put an end to its incursion into her domain. She protected what God placed under her authority. She knew which side she was on, and she wasn't going to play politics with evil. She killed it. Dead. Done.

You have been given a sphere of authority: your personal life, body, marriage, family, relationships, and the places and people God has given into your charge. Within that sphere, you are responsible for discerning what is coming in and going out. If it is evil, there is no compromise to make. If it is evil, there is no time to waste. If it is evil, you must act and kill it. Dead. Done. Go get your tent peg. *Dare to lead.*

Father, in Jesus' name, I am a leader who has a sphere of influence. You have given me authority over people and places in that sphere. I acknowledge my responsibility. Give me wisdom and discernment to know what is evil, the courage to act against it when it comes through the door of my tent, and Your love to lead well in every place in which You have given me authority. Amen!

DAY SIX:

You Are Wise

> Now the name of the man was Nabal, and the name of his wife
> Abigail. The woman was discerning.
>
> 1 Samuel 25:3–4

Abigail was a wise woman. When harm was determined against
her household, she saved her people by listening to the counsel
of a servant. She humbled herself before David on behalf of her
foolish husband, acting on behalf of the vulnerable, not seeking
and securing her welfare alone. She was discerning of the times,
perceiving what God was doing, declining to be politically motivated or manipulated. When she affirmed David as the anointed
of the Lord, she affirmed God's will, refusing to agree with the
fool and his foolish pride, superiority, and greed that blinded
him to the shift God was bringing. She yielded to the wisdom
and direction of God, cooperating sacrificially with the Spirit—
regardless of the cost to herself. This is the highest wisdom of all.

    You are a woman of God, which means that, like Abigail, you
have given your life in submission to Him and have the ability
through His Word, by His voice and Spirit, to discern the times.
You can perceive, practically and prophetically, what He is doing
in any given circumstance; therefore, cultivate selflessness, humility, and a listening ear, allowing every fiery opposition and

217

challenge to purify your heart and foster dependence upon God. In this way, you will be wise and called upon to partner in the move of God in your generation. *Be nobody's fool.*

PRAYER

Father, in the name of Jesus, I submit myself to You and Your Word, forgiving those who have behaved foolishly, bringing difficulty into my life. Grant that I grow in humility, grace, discernment, and selflessness, always being willing to listen and act for others. Give me understanding and insight to know what You are doing so that I can partner with You every day. Amen.

You Can Do Hard Things

> When she could hide him no longer, she took for him a basket. . . .
> put the child in it and placed it among the reeds by the river bank.
>
> Exodus 2:3

The future deliverer, Moses, needed deliverance. So Jochebed did the only thing she knew to do. She built an ark, put her baby inside, put it in the Nile, and let go. If she had for a moment tightened her grip instead of opening her hands and letting go of control over what she had given birth to, salvation might never have come. Not for Moses, not for her other children, not for her, not for Israel.

Her letting go facilitated God's purposes for Moses until the time of fulfillment of his calling; however, she could not have known that purpose. In her pain, she had to choose to let go. She opened her hand, relinquishing her right to a title, control, grandiosity, and self-centered ambition to humble herself as a servant for the sake of the life of another and the world as she knew it.

Godly women throughout history have done this hard thing of letting go. It requires *muchness*—the courage to entrust into God's hands what you give birth to; the humility to serve when you thought you would lead; the effort to be self-sacrificing, self-giving, and selfless when you want to cling, grab, be counted, be acknowledged, and climb the ladder of worldly success. It requires the courage to live openhandedly, without strings attached, regarding all the Lord has given you.

Finally, it requires incredible courage and faith that God can keep whatever you entrust to Him so that nothing good is ever lost, even if you have to let loose of it for a time. Any good thing that is loosed is never lost. And the very act of releasing unleashes the Spirit in your life for your good and the good of all those who are around you.

Girl, you *can* do hard things. *Let go*. Let God.

PRAYER

Father, I can only do hard things if You help me. So give me the courage to let go, to trust You, and to let You do what only You can do for the sake of the world. In Jesus' name, Amen.

You Are Saved, So Sing!

> He said to Simon, "Do you see this woman?"
>
> Luke 7:44

Simon was blind. His religious spirit deceived him into thinking he was superior. He judged the woman a sinner and Jesus a fraud. He could not see his own sin. The woman had been bound by both her sins and a religious spirit that shrouded her in shame. Finally, she meets Jesus, who makes her clean, whole, and new. The Pharisees never did that. Rescued from brokenness and the broken religious system, she offers worship that defies the religious spirit, refusing to skulk in the dark for fear of being called out for her sin.

The religious spirit in the Church places limitations on the identity and call on women's lives. In some regard, a stigma or veiled sense of shame is still attached to being female. But remember, no one is safe from being judged when in the presence of a religious spirit—not male or female, young or old, rich or poor, sick or well, strong or weak. And perhaps the surest sign of a religious spirit is that it attacks other religious spirits, shattering communities and neglecting those most in need in the effort to gain power and control over those it judges as its enemies.

In our story, the woman shows us the way forward, the way to avoid the temptations of religious spirits. She asks us to see beyond her forgiveness to her courageous worship. Like hers, our story doesn't end with seeing who Jesus is and the truth of all He has done. It continues with singing—with worship. The loudest song you can ever sing is to walk in your calling, without shame or apology, regardless of who is watching or judging. Fulfilling the call on your life, in the freedom that Jesus has given by the power of the Holy Spirit, is the most courageous and extravagant worship you can give to Him. It is the very thing that most deliberately and effectively *defies the religious spirits* of our day, even the subtlest and sneakiest ones that lurk inside of what might seem to be holy ideas and sacred beliefs. If you fulfill your calling, you'll become more and more like this woman—looking to Jesus and lavishing Him with thanksgiving and praise rather than looking at others in suspicion and blame.

PRAYER

Father, thank You for all You have done to save, heal, and deliver me. Give me the courage to worship You by walking in the call on my life without shame or apology, regardless of who is watching or judging. In doing so, I will defy the religious spirit! In Jesus' name, Amen.

You Have Permission

"Go into all the world and proclaim the gospel."

Mark 16:15

In Genesis, the blessing and calling of God are given equally and without hierarchy to both the man and the woman. God commissioned them to rule conjointly, creating woman for partnership with the man to receive the covenantal blessing of fruitfulness and fulfill the responsibility of having dominion over creation. This is how it was supposed to be, but sin and its consequences distorted their relationship.

Jesus came to restore all things. He lifts women out of the limitations and labels placed on them. In Acts, the Spirit is poured out on all disciples alike. Women in the New Testament serve as founders of churches, teachers, pastors, prophets, evangelists, and apostles. Paul, like Jesus, praises and supports Christian women who prophesy, teach, evangelize, preach, plant, and lead.[1] Scripture places no limits on what women can be called to do. *You have permission to be* me'od.

Throughout history, women have answered the call of God. Their hearts burned with passion for the lost, the broken, the sick, the poor, the widow, and the orphan. They looked at society and lifted their voices, offered their hands and feet, and laid down their lives to create something better, something holier, and something pleasing to the heart of God.

PRAYER

Father, You have given me permission to rise into the fullness of the call on my life. Please give me courage. Empower me by Your Spirit. Here I am, send me! In Jesus' name, Amen.

DAY TEN:

THE WORLD IS WAITING FOR YOU

The Lord gave the word; great was the company of those who
proclaimed it.

Psalm 68:11 NKJV

Girlfriend, you have been empowered by the Holy Spirit to slay
the devils and devilish systems of this world that loom large, like
giants of old, terrifying people—children, men, and women—
threatening to kill, steal, and destroy. The devil is a liar. Remember that the battle has been won. And God has a victory for you
to announce and a Gospel for you to proclaim.

There is a great company of bold, courageous, and cunning
women—women who have found their *muchness*—rising in our
day to sing, announce, and proclaim the Good News of Jesus.
The call went out from the very moment we were created. This
is our heritage and inheritance. The world is waiting. *Find your
muchness and rise into the fullness of the call!*

PRAYER

*Father, in the name of Jesus, I want my life to count for You
in this life with which You have gifted me. I want to stand
in the ranks of those faithful women portrayed in Scripture*

225

and throughout history who stormed the gates of hell, setting the captives free, whether they were friends or foes, family, neighbors, or strangers. I want to preach the Gospel and see bodies, hearts, and relationships healed. I want the courage to follow You wherever it leads me all the days of my life. Every day, every word, everything I am for You and the Kingdom, for all my life. Please show me the way. Show me how to love the way You love, holding nothing back. Heal my heart of anything that would hold me back. Remove from me anything that would make me stumble and lose my way. Please open my eyes to see, clearly and truly, what can only be seen by those who believe. Give me a whole heart so that I may offer You unbroken and undivided praise with undistracted and uncorrupted service. How I love You. How I praise You. How grateful I am for all You are and all You have given me. Amen.

NOTES

Dedication

1. "[A] fictional character, a ferocious monster described in the nonsense poem 'Jabberwocky,' which appears in the novel *Through the Looking Glass* (1871) by Lewis Carroll." The editors of *Encyclopaedia Brittanica*, "Jabberwock," Britannica.com, https://www.britannica.com/topic/Jabberwock.

Introduction

1. *Alice in Wonderland*, directed by Tim Burton, Walt Disney Productions, 2010.
2. Ibid., 37:38
3. Ibid., 38:04–38:18
4. Ibid., 38:22
5. "3966. Me'od," BibleHub.com, https://biblehub.com/hebrew/3966.htm.
6. Vinson Synan, *The Century of the Holy Spirit: 100 Years of Pentecostal and Charismatic Renewal* (Nashville: Thomas Nelson, 2001), 262.

Chapter One Throw Out the Bondwoman!

1. Megan Dalla-Camina, "The Reality of Imposter Syndrome," Psychology Today.com, September 3, 2018, https://www.psychologytoday.com/us/blog/real-women/201809/the-reality-imposter-syndrome.
2. Hebrews 11:11
3. Hebrews 11:12
4. Genesis 12:1–4; Hebrews 11:8
5. The story of Sarah's life can be found in Genesis 11:27–23:2.

6. God changed Abram's name to Abraham later in the story. As with Abraham, God changed Sarai's name to Sarah later in the story.
7. Genesis 11:30
8. Hebrews 11:1
9. Matthew 4:4 NKJV
10. Genesis 15:4
11. Genesis 15:6
12. Genesis 16:1
13. I have taken a bit of license here in the story to illustrate the point. In the biblical text we are not actually told what her motivation was, but we do know she took matters into her own hands instead of waiting on the Lord for supernatural intervention.
14. Matthew 12:34
15. Genesis 16:2
16. Genesis 16:2b
17. Genesis 16:4
18. Genesis 16:3–4
19. Genesis 16:5–6
20. Genesis 18:12
21. Genesis 18:13
22. "6381. Pala," BibleHub.com, https://biblehub.com/hebrew/6381.htm.
23. Isaiah 7:9 NIV
24. Genesis 21:8–9
25. "6711.Tsachaq," BibleHub.com, https://biblehub.com/hebrew/6711.htm.
26. Genesis 21:10
27. John 2:5 NKJV
28. Genesis 16:9–13; 21:13

Chapter Two Get in Position!

1. Psalm 121; Romans 8:28
2. Tom Wright, *Paul for Everyone: Romans Part 1: Chapters 1–8* (London: Society for Promoting Christian Knowledge, 2004), 156.
3. James 1:3
4. Hebrews 10:30–35
5. Carolyn Custis James, *The Gospel of Ruth: Loving God Enough to Break the Rules* (Grand Rapids: Zondervan, 2008), 26.
6. Judges 21:25
7. Robert L. Hubbard, *The Book of Ruth, The New International Commentary on the Old Testament* (Grand Rapids: Eerdmans, 1988), 85. In a footnote, Hubbard writes, "Famines sent Abram to Egypt (Gen. 12:10) and Isaac to Philistia (Gen. 26:1) where both experienced divine protection (esp. their wives) and emerged much wealthier than before. In my judgment, these episodes serve a thematic purpose in Genesis, namely, to mark them as men of a divinely guided

historical destiny. Similarly, famine drove Jacob and his sons to Egypt (Gen. 41–50) where their descendants also prospered and experienced the miraculous Exodus of a new nation, Israel (Exodus 1–20). Cf. 1 K. 17:1; Amos 8:11; Matt. 3:4; 4:2; Luke 15:14–17."

8. Ruth1:1–5

9. C. H. Spurgeon, "What Is a Revival?" Archive.Spurgeon.org, https://archive .spurgeon.org/s_and_t/wir1866.php.

10. Ruth 1:6

11. Henry Cloud, Facebook, June 23, 2017, https://www.facebook.com /DrHenryCloud/photos/a.489655829570/10155496476384571/?type=3#.

12. Hebrews 11:1 NKJV

13. Ruth 1:6–7

14. Ruth 1:8–9

15. Ruth 1:11–13

16. Job 10:1; 1 Samuel 30:6; 2 Kings 4:27

17. Carolyn Custis James, *Finding God in the Margins: The Book of Ruth*, ed. Craig G. Bartholomew et al., (Bellingham, WA: Transformative Word; Burlington, ON: Lexham Press, 2018), 27.

18. Hebrews 12:15

19. Ruth 1:14–15

20. Ruth 1:16–17

21. Genesis 12:1, Hebrews 11:8

22. Ruth 1:19

23. Ruth 1:20–21

24. Ruth 1:22 (emphasis added)

25. Romans 11:29

26. Ruth 1:22

27. Psalm 126

Chapter Three Speak Up

1. Matthew Henry, *Matthew Henry's Commentary on the Whole Bible: Complete and Unabridged in One Volume* (Peabody, MA: Hendrickson, 1994), 228.

2. Jason Koutsoukis, "India Burning Brides and Ancient Practice Is on the Rise," smh.com.au, https://www.smh.com.au/world/india-burning-brides-and -ancient-practice-is-on-the-rise-20150115-12r4j1.html.

3. Exodus 15:21

4. Numbers 1:2–3

5. Numbers 13:31

6. Numbers 14:4

7. Numbers 26:51

8. Hebrews 11:8

9. Numbers 26:33

10. Numbers 26:52–56

11. Matthew 1:1
12. Numbers 27:1–4
13. "Meaning of Numbers in the Bible: The Number 5," BibleStudy.org, https://www.biblestudy.org/bibleref/meaning-of-numbers-in-bible/5.html.
14. Ecclesiastes 4:9–12
15. Hemchand Gossai, "Dowry," *Eerdmans Dictionary of the Bible*, ed. David Freedman, Allen C. Myers, and Astrid B. Beck (Grand Rapids: Eerdmans, 2000), 355.
16. Numbers 22:2
17. Numbers 22–24
18. Numbers 25
19. Numbers 14:4; 27:4. Avivah Gottlieb Zornberg, following the thinking of Rashi, a French eleventh-century commentator who uses this Hebrew word play to make the point that women in Exodus narratives loved the land of Israel, thus survived the wilderness not being destroyed along with the apostate men. Interesting thought. Avivah Gottlieb Zornberg, *The Particulars of Rapture: Reflections on the Exodus* (New York: Shocken, 2001), 7–8.
20. Hebrews 11
21. Numbers 27:3–4
22. 1 Kings 16–21; 2 Kings 9
23. Numbers 27:7–11
24. When the five daughters of Zelophehad declared their rights and won a court decision, they put in place a law that is recognized to this day. Known as "the oldest decided case," it is still turned to for opinions and is "cited as an authority" by the American Bar Association. In the February 1924 *American Bar Association Journal*, Henry C. Clark quoted the decision of the daughters of Zelophehad as "an early declaratory judgment in which the property rights of women marrying outside of their tribe are clearly set forth." Henry C. Clark, in "Daughters of Zelophehad: Bible's First Feminists," Daily-Journal.com, https://www.daily-journal.com/life/religion/daughters-of-zelophehad-bibles-first-feminists/article_2db45c85-a25e-5329-a0c1-23c9e85b6f9d.html#.
25. Ephesians 3:20
26. *The Little Mermaid*, directed by Ron Clements and John Musker, Walt Disney Studios, 1989.
27. Hebrews 1:1–3
28. Diane Langberg, *Redeeming Power: Understanding Authority and Abuse in the Church* (Grand Rapids: Brazos Press, 2020), 139.

Chapter Four Dare to Lead!

1. Judges 4:9 NIV, emphasis added
2. David Vergun, "Rosie the Riveter Inspired Women to Serve in World War II," Defense.gov, https://www.defense.gov/News/Feature-Stories/story/Article/1791664/rosie-the-riveter-inspired-women-to-serve-in-world-war-ii/.

3. Kay Bailey Hutchison, *American Heroines: The Spirited Women Who Shaped Our Country* (New York: Harper, 2004). Inscription on the WWII Memorial for Colonel Oveta Culp Hobby.
4. "Case Study: Always #LikeAGirl," CampaignLive.co.uk, 2015, https://www.campaignlive.co.uk/article/case-study-always-likeagirl/1366870.
5. Ibid.
6. Joshua 2
7. Esther 4–9
8. 2 Samuel 20
9. 1 Samuel 25
10. Judges 4–5
11. Judges 5:6–7
12. Acts 2; Joel 2:28–29; Isaiah 59:19–21; Jeremiah 31:33
13. 1 Corinthians 12
14. Hebrews 2:4
15. Judges 4:4–5
16. Judges 4:4
17. Brandon Grafius, "Deborah the Judge," in *The Lexham Bible Dictionary*, ed. John D. Barry et al. (Bellingham, WA: Lexham Press, 2016).
18. M. A. Seifrid, "Righteousness, Justice, and Justification," in *New Dictionary of Biblical Theology*, ed. T. Desmond Alexander, and Brian S. Rosner (Downers Grove, IL: InterVarsity Press, 2000), 742.
19. Judges 4:17
20. "Enjoli Perfume," 1982, https://www.youtube.com/watch?v=3N9K7eoVtm0&themeRefresh=1.
21. Nava Atlas, "How Harriet Beecher Stowe Was Inspired to Write *Uncle Tom's Cabin*," LiteraryLadiesGuide.com, https://www.literaryladiesguide.com/literary-musings/how-harriet-beecher-stowe-was-inspired-to-write-uncle-toms-cabin/.
22. Amelia Costigan, "The Double-Bind Dilemma for Women in Leadership," Catalyst.org, August 2, 2018, https://www.catalyst.org/research/infographic-the-double-bind-dilemma-for-women-in-leadership/.
23. Helen E. Fisher, "The Natural Leadership Talents of Women," in *Enlightened Power: How Women Are Transforming the Practice of Leadership*, ed. Linda Coughlin, Ellen Wingard, Keith Hollihan (San Francisco: Jossey-Bass, 2005), 134–136.
24. Ibid.
25. Ibid.
26. Nicolas D. Kristoff, and Sheryl WuDunn, *Half the Sky: Turning Oppression into Opportunity for Women* Worldwide (New York: Vintage Books, 2010), xix–xx.
27. Judges 5:7 NASB
28. Isaiah 49:15
29. Julia Ward Howe, "Appeal to Womanhood Throughout the World," Boston, September 1870, https://www.loc.gov/resource/rbpe.07400300/.

30. "History of Mother's Day," NationalWomensHistoryAlliance.org. Julie Ward Howe, "A Proclamation for Mother's Day," NCChurches.org, https://nationalwomenshistoryalliance.org/resources/commemorations/history-of-mothers-day/.
31. Julie Ward Howe, "A Proclamation for Mother's Day," NCChurches.org, https://ncchurches.org/wp-content/uploads/2010/07/Mothers-Day-for-Peace-2008b.pdf.
32. Judges 5:6–7
33. Judges 5:28–30
34. Genesis 1:28
35. John Wesley, *Explanatory Notes upon the Old Testament, Vol. 1.* (Bristol: William Pine, 1765).

Chapter Five Be Nobody's Fool!

1. 1 Samuel 25:1
2. Ecclesiastes 3
3. Psalm 139:16 NIV
4. Isaiah 43:19, emphasis added
5. Genesis 1:27
6. 1 Samuel 15:26–28
7. 1 Samuel 18:7
8. 1 Samuel 25:3
9. Leonard Greenspoon, "Abigail, Wife of David," *The Lexham Bible Dictionary*, ed. John D. Barry et al. (Bellingham, WA: Lexham Press, 2016).
10. Some scholars believe this to be a sort of insult regarding his character or attitude, others his descendancy. I have chosen to go with lineage.
11. Joshua 14:6–14
12. Genesis 12:1–3
13. Proverbs 14:16; 18:12; Psalm 53:1. Scripture has much to say about the fool in contrast to the wise. Do a search of the word *fool* in your favorite Bible app to get a fuller understanding.
14. 1 Samuel 25:8
15. 1 Samuel 25:10–11
16. Proverbs 1:32 KJV
17. Deuteronomy 8:11–20
18. 1 Samuel 25:14–17, emphasis added
19. Proverbs 1:20–29
20. 1 Samuel 30:1–20
21. "De'ah," BibleStudyTools.com, https://www.biblestudytools.com/lexicons/hebrew/kjv/deah.html.
22. "7200.Raah," BibleHub.com, https://www.biblestudytools.com/lexicons/hebrew/kjv/deah.html.
23. Genesis 16:13

24. Luke 16
25. Luke 16:8
26. Shrewdness involves critical judgment with prophetic insight and fore-sight. Isaiah compares those who bow down to a block of wood to those who are not shrewd. Can a block of wood be a god simply because it is carved into one? In contemporary terms, can having five thousand friends on Facebook give me true community? The answer to both is no. To believe so would not be shrewd. Shrewdness is what Paul assumes we all have when he says, "I speak as to shrewd men, judge for yourselves what I am saying!" Being shrewd, we don't judge hearts. Rather, we judge fruit, situations, policies, and philosophies coming to wise conclusions. Shrewdness is what Jesus expects of His disciples when He says, "Behold, I send you out as sheep among wolves, so be shrewd as serpents, and innocent as doves." You see, there is a mission. We are all are being sent out to gather the harvest and expand the Kingdom. The mission takes place in a hostile world where the Kingdom of God suffers violence. In this kind of world, we are to be as shrewd as serpents and innocent as doves. Why a serpent? To understand this, we must look at the first serpent, the one in the Garden of Eden. Genesis describes that serpent as crafty—the most cunning beast created. In other words (from examining the Hebrew language), the serpent was shrewd. He saw the big picture, and he acted to redirect the outcome. The serpent understood man was made in God's image and had been given dominion over everything. He was after that dominion. He had come against God and was thrown to the earth. Now he would come against God's image, against humanity, to take dominion over God's creation to become lord of the age. He was shrewd. We are charged by Jesus to be as shrewd as a serpent: to see the big picture, which means to see and assess what is going on as well as what will come because of what is going on so that we may act in order to redirect the outcome on behalf of the Kingdom. If only Adam and Eve had been shrewd in the Garden. Yet, what was lost, Jesus has taken back and gives to us once more. Will we be shrewd? Will we be not only shrewd, but also innocent? Paul warns us to be shrewd as to what is good, but innocent as to what is evil, meaning whatever is the work of the flesh and darkness. Why? Because without the right heart and pure motives led by the Holy Spirit in submission to God's will and mission, shrewd becomes a snake. We act in manipulative, selfish, self-seeking, underhanded, and undermining ways. Yet, without shrewdness, innocence is naïve and gullible.
27. *Hidden Figures*, directed by Theodore Melfi, Twentieth Century Fox, 2016.
28. 1 Samuel 25:19
29. 1 Samuel 25:28–31, emphasis added
30. 1 Samuel 25:37–39
31. Wedding at Cana, John 2:1–12
32. 1 Samuel 16:7
33. 1 Samuel 25:31

Chapter Six Let Go

1. Tikva Frymer-Kensky, *Reading the Women of the Bible: A New Interpretation of Their Stories* (New York: Random House, 2002), 24.
2. Genesis 46:3 KJV
3. Genesis 15:5; 17:5–6
4. Genesis 1:28
5. Exodus 1:7 ASV
6. Isaiah 55:10–11; Hebrews 4:12; 6:13–18
7. Genesis 15:13–14
8. Genesis 15:14
9. "Irony," Merriam-Webster.com, https://www.merriam-webster.com/thesaurus/irony.
10. Iain D. Campbell, "Opening Up Exodus," *Opening Up Commentary* (Leominster: Day One Publications, 2006), 26.
11. A rabbinic Midrash explains, "Rather, they told Pharaoh that this nation is like the beasts (*hayyot*) of the field; the women, who are like beasts, do not need the help of any human. Thus, in Jacob's blessing to his sons in Gen. 49, Judah is compared to a lion's whelp, Dan to a serpent, Naphtali to a hind let loose, Issachar to a strong-boned ass, and so forth." Tamar Kadari, "Jochebed: Midrash and Aggadah," JWA.org, https://jwa.org/encyclopedia/article/shiphrah-midrash-and-aggadah. See also Fryer-Kensky, *Reading*, 25.
12. Exodus 1:20–21
13. David Jobling, and Tina Pippin, eds. "The Hebrew Women Are Not Like the Egyptian Women: The Ideology of Race, Gender, and Sexual Reproduction in Exodus I," *Semeia* 59 (Atlanta: Society of Biblical Literature, 1992), 32.
14. Exodus 1:22
15. Exodus 2:1–2
16. 2 Samuel 20
17. 1 Kings 17:8–16
18. Mark 5:25–34
19. John 4
20. Tamar Kadari, "Jochebed: Midrash and Aggadah," JWA.org, https://jwa.org/encyclopedia/article/jochebed-midrash-and-aggadah.
21. "Shiphrah," Sefaria.org, https://www.sefaria.org/search?q=shiphrah&tab=text&tvar=1&tsort=relevance&svar=1&ssort=relevance.
22. Hebrews 11:7
23. "What Is Midrash?" MyJewishLearning.com, https://www.myjewishlearning.com/article/midrash-101/.
24. Tamar Kadari, "Jochebed: Midrash and Aggadah." JWA.org, https://jwa.org/encyclopedia/article/jochebed-midrash-and-aggadah.
25. Ecclesiastes 3:6b
26. Exodus 2:4
27. Exodus 2:11

28. Exodus 2:5–10
29. Luke 1:38
30. Luke 2:34–35
31. Acts 1:14
32. John 20:17–18
33. Isaiah 43:1–2
34. "This exegesis teaches of Jochebed's longevity, and that she was still alive when Moses died. This is corroborated by another early Midrash that states that Jochebed was one of the offspring of Jacob who went down to Egypt and was also among those who entered the land of Canaan (*Seder Olam Rabbah* 9)." Tamar Kadari, "Jochebed: Midrash and Aggadah," JWA.org, https://jwa.org /encyclopedia/article/jochebed-midrash-and-aggadah.

Chapter Seven Defy the Religious Spirit

1. John Newton, "Amazing Grace," 1779.
2. Luke 7
3. James 1:23–24
4. Acts 1:1
5. Luke 17:11–19
6. Luke 17:17
7. Luke 5:30
8. I. Howard Marshall, *The Gospel of Luke: A Commentary on the Greek Text, New International Greek Testament Commentary* (Exeter: Paternoster, 1978), 302.
9. Joel B. Green, *The Gospel of Luke, The New International Commentary on the New Testament* (Grand Rapids: Eerdmans, 1997).
10. See chapter 2 in *The Way of the Kingdom* for a more extensive treatment of "offense." About putting God on trial, C. S. Lewis explains, "The ancient man approached God (or even the gods) as the accused person approaches his judge. For the modern man, the roles are quite reversed. He is the judge: God is in the dock. He is quite a kindly judge; if God should have a reasonable defense for being the god who permits war, poverty, and disease, he is ready to listen to it. The trial may even end in God's acquittal. But the important thing is that man is on the bench and God is in the dock." C. S. Lewis, ed. Walter Hooper, "God in the Dock." *God in the Dock: Essays on Theology and Ethics* (Grand Rapids: Eerdmans, 1970), LOC 3098 (Kindle); Kim Maas, *The Way of the Kingdom: Seizing the Moment for a Great Move of God* (Grand Rapids: Chosen Books, 2021).
11. Luke 7:33–35
12. Luke 7:36
13. Matthew 5:45; Acts 10:34–35; Romans 2:11; 2 Peter 3:9
14. James Swanson, *Dictionary of Biblical Languages with Semantic Domains: Greek (New Testament)* (Oak Harbor: Logos Research Systems, 1997).

15. Matthew 8:31; Mark 9:17; Luke 9:1; 10:17; 11:14; 1 Corinthians 10:20
16. Luke 7:37–38
17. N. J. Opperwall, "Sinner." *The International Standard Bible Encyclopedia, Revised*, ed. Geoffrey W. Bromiley (Grand Rapids: Eerdmans, 1988), 529; Karl Heinrich Rengstorf, "Ἁμαρτωλός, Ἀναμάρτητος," *Theological Dictionary of the New Testament*, ed. Gerhard Kittel, Geoffrey W. Bromiley, and Gerhard Friedrich, vol. 1 (Grand Rapids: Eerdmans, 1964), 328.
18. Luke 7:39
19. Luke 7:24–30
20. Luke 7:40–43
21. Matthew 23:1–36
22. Luke 7:44–48
23. Luke 7:49
24. Abraham Joshua Heschel, *The Insecurity of Freedom* (New York: Macmillan, 1956), 181, emphasis added.
25. Luke 7:49
26. Linda Esposito, "Why Do We Repeat the Past in Our Relationships?" PsychologyToday.com, March 22, 2016, https://www.psychologytoday.com/us/blog/anxiety-zen/201603/why-do-we-repeat-the-past-in-our-relationships.
27. John 4:7–42

Chapter Eight Permission to Be *Me'od*—For the Sake of the World

1. John 4:28–29
2. Mark 16:15 NIV
3. Mel Schwartz, "Defining Moments," Psychology.com, September 24, 2008, http://www.psychology.com/articles/?p=18.
4. John 4
5. John 4:4
6. John 4:27–38
7. John 4:7, emphasis added
8. John 4:16, emphasis added
9. John 4:21, emphasis added
10. John 4:25–26
11. Roberta Hestenes, "The Woman at the Well: Jesus and the Ministry of Women," *Priscilla Papers* 12, no. 1 (1998).
12. Tom Brady, "I didn't come this far to only come this far, so we've still got further to go," 247Sports.com, https://247sports.com/Player/76179/Quotes/I-didnt-come-this-far-to-only-come-this-far-so-weve-still-got-fu-45570346/. (Yes, I love football, and yes, I think Tom Brady is the G.O.A.T—greatest of all time.)
13. Genesis 1:26–28
14. Genesis 2:18
15. Deuteronomy 33:26–29

16. Carl Schultz, "1598 עָזַר" *Theological Wordbook of the Old Testament*, ed. R. Laird Harris, Gleason L. Archer Jr., and Bruce K. Waltke (Chicago: Moody Press, 1999), 660–661; Victor P. Hamilton, "The Book of Genesis, Chapters 1–17," *The New International Commentary on the Old Testament* (Grand Rapids: Eerdmans, 1990), 175–176; Gordon J. Wenham, "Genesis," in *Eerdmans Commentary on the Bible*, ed. James D. G. Dunn and John W. Rogerson (Grand Rapids; Cambridge, U.K.: Eerdmans, 2003), 40.

17. Wes Pinkham and Christopher D. Waters, *Identity Formation: The Journey Toward Personhood*. Self-published. Relational Theology Lecture Materials, 2001, 187–189.

18. Genesis 3:12–19

19. Luke 10:38–42

20. N. T. Wright, "The Biblical Basis for Women's Service in the Church," *Priscilla Papers* 20, no. 4 (Autumn 2006), 7.

21. According to Kevin Giles, it is likely that the Twelve were men because they were to be the "founding fathers of the new Israel they were the counterparts of the twelve male patriarchs, and because they were to be 'witnesses' of the life ministry, death, and resurrection of Jesus, something women could not legitimately do in Jewish society at that time," as Josephus explicitly states in Ant. 4:219. See likewise Rabbi Akiba, m.Yeb. 15:1. Giles, Kevin. "Post-1970s Evangelical Responses to the Emancipation of Women," *Priscilla Papers* 20, no. 4, 2006, 49–52.

22. N. T. Wright, "The Biblical Basis for Women's Service in the Church," *Priscilla Papers* 20, no. 4 (Autumn 2006), 7.

23. Luke 24:49

24. Joel 2:28–29; Isaiah 59:18–21; Jeremiah 31:33–34; Numbers 11:29; Ezekiel 11:19–20

25. Acts 2:14–38; Isaiah 59:21

26. Hebrews 2:3–4

27. Estrelda Alexander and Amos Young, *Philip's Daughters: Women in Pentecostal-Charismatic Leadership* (Eugene, OR: Pickwick Publications, 2009), 136.

28. John 3:8 KJV

29. House churches were the *only* kind of churches at that time in the first century. Lydia (Acts 16:13–15), Chloe (1 Cor 1:11, 4:12), Nympha (Col 4:15), Apphia (Philemon 2).

30. Paul calls a woman, Junia, an outstanding apostle (Rom 16:7). Junias was a translation given by history. It reveals no evidence of such a name for a man, though Junia, a woman's name, is common. Chrysostom used Junia in his rendering, and it was not until the thirteenth century that Junia was changed to Junias. Phoebe, a "servant" or deacon and leader of a house church, and Priscilla, the teacher of Apollos and a fellow worker, which is a term used for other male leaders (see Romans 16:3–4).

31. 1 Peter 2:4–5:9

32. Revelation 1:6; 5:10; 20:6

33. Galatians 3:28

34. 1 Corinthians 11–14

35. Kevin Giles, "Post-1970s Evangelical Responses to the Emancipation of Women," *Priscilla Papers* 20, no. 4, (Autumn 2006), 49–52.

36. Craig S. Keener, *Paul, Women, & Wives: Marriage and Women's Ministry in the Letters of Paul* (Peabody, MA: Hendrickson, 1992), 88.

37. Ibid.

38. Ibid.

39. Tom Wright, *Paul for Everyone: The Pastoral Letters: 1 and 2 Timothy and Titus* (London: Society for Promoting Christian Knowledge, 2004), 26.

40. Romans 16:3–4, 7; 1 Corinthians 4:12; Colossians 4:15; Philemon 2

41. "The Foursquare Church Celebrates 100 Years of Ministry," Religion News.com, December 21, 2022, https://religionnews.com/2022/12/21/the-foursquare-church-celebrates-100-years-of-ministry/#.

42. Vinson Synan, *The Holiness-Pentecostal Tradition: Charismatic Movements in the Twentieth Century* (Grand Rapids: Eerdmans, 1997), 203.

43. Florence Nightingale, "Florence Nightingale Quotes," GoodReads.com, https://www.goodreads.com/quotes/265726-if-i-could-give-you-information-of-my-life-it.

Conclusion

1. Lewis Carroll, *Alice's Adventures in Wonderland and Through the Looking Glass* (New York: Harper Design, 2019), 227.

2. Psalm 68:11 NKJV

3. Tim Burton, *Alice in Wonderland*, Walt Disney Studios Motion Pictures, 2010, 1:25:57–1:27:57.

4. Psalm 68:11 NKJV

5. Luke 1:46–55

Devotional Day Nine You Have Permission

1. Romans 16:3–4, 7; 1 Corinthians 4:12; Colossians 4:15; Philemon 2

KIM MAAS is a sought-after international speaker, author, and minister. After a radical encounter with the Holy Spirit on March 22, 1994, Kim left her 22-year nursing career to serve God full-time. Her passion is for people to gain confidence in who God is and what He says so that they can move forward. She is called to go into all the world to preach and prophesy the Word of God with signs and wonders following, equipping, and educating the Body of Christ for local and global Kingdom advancement. Kim served as a pastor in the local church for many years before becoming a full-time itinerant minister. She is the president and CEO of Kim Maas Ministries, founder of Women of Our Time, host of the *Move Forward with Dr. Kim Maas* podcast and *Voice of the Shepherds* podcast, and the *Move Forward with Dr. Kim Maas* TV program on KiTV and Vision TV Houston. Kim is the author of *Prophetic Community: God's Call for All to Minister in His Gifts* and *The Way of the Kingdom: Seizing the Moment for a Great Move of God*, published by Chosen Books. She has also authored several self-published resources for personal and group studies. Kim is ordained with the Apostolic Network of Global Awakening and licensed with her home church, Heart of the City. She earned a doctorate in ministry at United Theological Seminary and a master of divinity at King's University. Kim and her husband, Mike, live in Northern Idaho. They have three married children and a growing number of grandchildren.

You can connect with Kim at www.kimmaas.com, on Instagram @kimmaasministries, on Facebook @MoveforwardNow KimMaas, on Twitter @pkmaas, and by email at hello@kimmaas .com.